KOYA: AN OUTLINE GRAMMAR
Gommu Dialect

INDIA
·Nagpur
Hyderabad·
Godavari River
Koya Habitat

KOYA:
AN OUTLINE GRAMMAR

Gommu Dialect

BY

STEPHEN A. TYLER

UNIVERSITY OF CALIFORNIA PRESS
BERKELEY AND LOS ANGELES
1969

UNIVERSITY OF CALIFORNIA PUBLICATIONS IN LINGUISTICS

Volume 54

Approved for publication March 28, 1968
Issued January 17, 1969
Price, $3.50

University of California Press
Berkeley and Los Angeles
California

University of California Press, Ltd.
London, England

Manufactured in the United States of America

PREFACE

The data for this grammar were collected in 1962 and 1963 in the course of a year's ethnographic field work among the Koyas. Relatively few of the usual linguistic texts are used. The majority of my texts deal with Koya social organization. They are the result of an instruction to the informant to "tell me a story about Koya weddings, divorce, sacrifices, festivals, gods, origins, etc." Statements occurring in these texts were then used as linguistic frames in the construction of questions about Koya culture. The texts then, served a dual purpose—they provided a corpus of data for linguistic analysis and a reference source for the construction of culturally relevant questions. A portion of these texts will be published as part of an ethnographic description now in preparation.

My principal informant was Pūsam Laksmayya of Pedda Nallaballi, Bhadrachallam Taluq, Khammam District, Andhra Pradesh. Laksmayya, a man some fifty years old, is a member of one of the two dominant lineages in Pedda Nallaballi and a highly respected elder in the village. Yet, he is atypical in some ways. He is a Christian and he is educated (SSLC). Paradoxically, these features which made him different also proved to be a distinct advantage. He is not only a Koya, he is also partially an outsider. Consequently, he could speak without restraint on features of Koya life that other informants were reluctant to talk about. Since he is bilingual in Koya and Telugu, the early stages of work involved a tri-lingual process of translation from Koya to Telugu to English. During this period I had the able assistance of my wife Martha and my Telugu assistant, Mr. Prasada Rao of Dummagudem. As work progressed I was eventually able to elicit information directly in Koya—albeit rather slowly. In the beginning I also had the use of a word list and Koya translation of First John and the Gospel According to Luke prepared in the latter part of the nineteenth century by Reverend John Cain. Almost all previous information on Koyas derives from Reverend Cain's early efforts (see Bibliography under Cain). In general, Cain's transcription of Koya (using Telugu characters) is sound. The only major differences between these early texts and my own are the somewhat higher percentage of Telugu loan words and the rather "literary" character of the Cain texts.

In the course of studies and research leading to the writing of this grammar, I have received assistance from numerous teachers, officials, friends, and last but not least, the Koyas themselves. Professors Alan R. Beals of Stanford University and A. Kimball Romney of Harvard, through long hours of conferences and a host of suggestions, assisted me in planning the research. Professor B. Gerow of Stanford guided my first real assays into linguistics and Dravidian languages while Professor Charles O. Frake, also of Stanford, made me aware of the uses of linguistic procedures in ethnography. Other

Stanford professors, notably B. Seigel and G. D. Spindler, also gave of their time and advice—as well as moral support. Professor C. von Fürer-Haimendorf of the School of Oriental and African Studies of the University of London very kindly wrote letters of introduction for me and from his vast fund of information on the tribes of Hyderabad, was able to give many useful suggestions and leads for research. I am also indebted to Professor M. B. Emeneau, Professor David L. Olmsted, Professor John Gumperz, Professor H. F. Schiffman, and Professor Jan Brukman for comments and suggestions on previous drafts.

While we were in the field, many friends and acquaintances in India aided us at various times. Professor Vyās Tirtha of Osmania University and his wife, Lālitha, were helpful in many ways during our first weeks in India. The officials of Osmania University very kindly extended affiliation with the university, and made the resources of the faculty and library available on several occasions. They were also instrumental in providing me with letters of introduction to various government officials and departments. Mr. V. Pratap of the Tribal Institute in Hyderabad briefed me on tribal conditions and governmental activities in Andhra Pradesh. In the tribal area, Mr. B. V. V. Murty, Superintendent of Schools in Burgumpahad Taluq gave many useful suggestions on Koya language and culture, and the Forestry Department allowed us to use their travelers' bungalows on several occasions. Of these friends and acquaintances, none were more valued than the Christian Missionary Society missionaries of Khammamet and Dummagudem. Particularly, Mr. Larry Pullen, Captain and Mrs. Phillip Hayne, and Miss Margaret Woods helped us in acquiring assistants, housing, and on more than one occasion—food.

My principal informant, Pūsam Laksmayya, was of more assistance than I can even begin to chronicle. His constant concern for the correctness of information on Koyas was a useful check on my sometimes misguided enthusiasms. Mr. Prasada Rao of Dummagudem was a loyal and conscientious helper, who willingly shared in the privations of some of my tours, and by his knowledge of local customs considerably eased my way. The good-natured humor with which Koyas abided my prying questions and halting efforts to speak Koya is a tribute to their tolerance.

I gratefully acknowledge the financial support given me by the Ford Foundation and the Faculty Research Committee of the University of California, Davis.
Lastly, I wish to acknowledge the assistance of my wife Martha. Her patience with my preoccupation with things Koya has been outstanding, and her willingness to share in the hardships of life in a rather remote tribal area made my work much easier. In addition, she actively assisted me in collecting linguistic and cultural data, and in the endless job of filing, copying, and cataloging.

Although all of these people have helped me in numerous ways, any mistakes, errors, and misconceptions in this grammar are strictly my own and cannot be attributed to them.

S. A. T.

CONTENTS

SYMBOLS

(X)	X is optional (in formulas)
(X)	X is morphemic (in utterances)
[X]	X is phonetic
/X/	X is phonemic
//X//	X is a cover symbol or morphophonemic
X_i X_j	Values of X, $i = j$ or $i \neq j$
X ~ Y	X varies with Y
X → Y	X is realized as (replaced by) Y
/___X//	In the environment of X
+	Internal juncture
#	Word juncture
	Terminal juncture
+ X	Plus X (in formulas)
± X	With or without X
$\begin{Bmatrix} X \\ Y \end{Bmatrix}$	X or Y
C	Consonant
V	Vowel

For an explanation of morphophonemic cover symbols see page 34, paragraph 2.20. For an explanation of other symbols and abbreviations see Appendices B and C.

Chapter I

INTRODUCTION

1.1. The Koyas occupy a 200-by-40-mile stretch of land on either side of the Godavari River in Andhra Pradesh, Madhya Pradesh, and Orissa. Government census data recorded on the basis of mother tongue in 1931, though unreliable in details, gave the distribution for states and districts shown in table 1.

TABLE 1

Koya Population Distribution (1931)

District	Male	Female	Total Koyas
Vizagapatnam	11,070	10,696	21,766
East Godavari	28,123	27,774	55,897
West Godavari	692	654	1,346
Totals	39,885	39,124	79,209

The taluk breakdown for each of these districts for both Agency and plains areas is given in table 2.

TABLE 2

Koya Population Breakdown by Taluk (1931)

District	Taluk	Number of Koyas
Vizagapatnam	Malkanagiri	19,854
	Pottangi	1,446
East Godavari	Bhadrachalam	34,058
	Chodavaram	10,041
	Nugur	2,687
	Polavaram	17,426
	Yellavaram	7,808
West Godavari	Chintalapudi	982
	All other	431

In addition to the 79,209 Koyas reported for Madras Presidency, 33,638 were reported for Hyderabad. Although census data for Koyas in Bastar (Madhya Pradesh) are unavailable for 1931, Grigson has estimated their number as between 6,000 and 9,000 (Grigson, 1938:53-55). No data were reported for Orissa in 1931.

Data from the 1941 census are difficult to compare with the 1931 figures owing to changes in methods of recording and redistricting. The state distributions for 1941 are given in table 3, with rough comparisons to 1931.

TABLE 3

Distribution of Koyas by State

State	1931	1941
Hyderabad	33,638	31,094
Orissa	---	27,000
Madras	79,209	95,633
Madhya Pradesh	6,000*	6,000*
Totals	118,847	159,727

*Grigson's estimate.

It is impossible to tell whether the increase of 18,000 Koyas in Madras and the decrease of 2,000 in Hyderabad represent real changes in population or differences in methods of recording. That something is awry is indicated by the 1941 figures for Madras districts, as shown in table 4.

TABLE 4

Distribution of Koyas by Districts in Madras

District	1931	1941
Vizagapatnam	21,766	320
East Godavari	55,897	90,959
West Godavari	1,346	1,717
Totals	79,209	92,996

The additional 40,000 Koyas in East Godavari probably represent most of the 20,000 lost in Vizagapatnam through differences in recording and redistricting, but this still leaves 20,000 unaccounted for. Whether other groups were recorded as Koyas in the 1941 census, or whether this represents population growth is unknown.

I have not had access to figures for the 1911, 1921, and 1951 censuses, but the 1961 handbook gives the following totals for those years:

1911	49,943
1921	21,492
1951	99,522

These figures refer only to Koya speakers in what is now Andhra Pradesh.

The 1961 census figures for Koya speakers are given in table 5.

TABLE 5

Koya Population Distribution (1961)

State	Male	Female	Total Koyas
Andhra Pradesh*	54,142	54,516	108,658
Orissa	15,570	15,482	31,052
Totals	69,712	69,998	139,710

*Census data for 1931 and 1941 refer to districts and states as constituted before the formation of Andhra Pradesh. All the districts formerly recorded in the Madras Presidency and Hyderabad state are now included in Andhra Pradesh. Most of the Agency part of East Godavari District is now included in the recently organized Khammam District. The 1961 census also lists 578 males and 374 females in Assam; 26 males and 19 females in Maharashtra; 23 males and 46 females in West Bengal; and 1 male in Nagaland. Except for those listed in Maharashtra these are all probably tea plantation employees. Including these figures the 1961 total is 140,777.

No figures are given for Koya speakers in Madhya Pradesh, but 35,455 persons were returned as speakers of Dorli. It seems likely that this figure either refers to Dorla Koyas or includes a substantial number of Koya speakers. Whether Dorli is a Koya dialect or a dialect of Gondi is unknown, but from my brief tours in Bastar it is evident that there is a large Koya-speaking population in that district. Consequently, I think it is safe to speculate that there are now probably 160,000 to 170,000 Koya speakers in India. With the extension of health services in recent years there has probably been a slight population increase, but whether this has been offset by acculturated Koyas counted as Telugu castes is not known.[1]

Even these figures are incomplete; they do indicate that the major areas of Koya concentration are along the alluvial plain of the Godavari River and in the uplands immediately behind it. In this area the largest concentrations are in Andhra Pradesh and especially in Bhadrachallam district.

1.2. Along the Godavari River and near major roads the Koyas live in contact with Telugu-speaking castes. To the north, along the Bastar border, they are in contact with various Gondi-speaking tribes and Indo-Aryan-speaking Hindu castes. Consequently, most Koya males are bilingual, speaking Koya and Telugu or Koya and one or another Hindi dialect. In more remote areas the majority of females speak only Koya with a minimum of bazaar Telugu, Hindi, or Oriya. Since Koya is a Gondi language, it is mutually intelligible with Hill Maria Gondi in Bastar and Sironcha. Though I have no real evidence, the general pattern seems to be for geographically adjacent Koya and Gondi populations to speak different, but mutually intelligible Gondi dialects. Where these populations are geographically non-contiguous, the dialects are not mutually intelligible. This same pattern probably prevails among all Gondi dialects..

[1]The 1931 census data are from Yeatts, 1932:279, 306. The 1941 data are from Government of India, 1942:308-312. The 1961 data are from Mitra, 1964:xv, cci, ccxxxv, 107.

1.3. Koyas of Bhadrachallam Taluk generally say there are three different kinds of Koyas—Gommu Koyas, Guṭṭa Koyas, and Lingu or Rāj Koyas. To this list some informants added Bāsa Koyas, Dōra or Dōrla Koyas, Reddis, and Naikpods. Gommu Koyas include all Koyas living in the Godavari plain and nearby hills. Guṭṭa Koyas occupy the higher, more remote hills in the border area between Bastar and Andhra Pradesh. Lingu Koyas are found mainly in Warangal district. Reddis occupy a rather small area near the Godavari gorge in Bhadrachallam, Burgumpahad, and Rampa Chodavaram. The Naikpods are concentrated at the opposite, up-river end of the Koya area with only scattered groups appearing in Bhadrachallam. Bāsa Koyas seem to include only those Koyas living in the plateau on the southern side of the Godavari River. Dōra or Dōrla Koyas are found in Malkanagiri and Bastar.

On the basis of linguistic evidence alone, Naikpods and Reddis are not Koyas. The Reddis speak Telugu, and the Naikpods are reputed to have their own language. There is some intermarriage between Koyas, Naikpods, and Reddis, but it is relatively infrequent (cf. Fürer-Haimendorf, 1945:240-243). Social organization also differs greatly between Reddis and Koyas. The Reddis, for example, do not have named patrilineages organized on a phratry basis as do the Koyas (Fürer-Haimendorf, 1945:148-178). The Naikpods present a slightly different problem. While those few I encountered in Bhadrachallam insisted that their people centered in Adilabad, I was unable to find many points of similarity between their social organization and that described in published sources (e.g., Fürer-Haimendorf, 1948:37-39). In addition, those I met spoke only Telugu. Koyas consider Naikpods to be the offspring of the sister of a Koya woman. Both sisters were wives of Bhīma. The Naikpods of Bhadrachallam are highly Teluguized, no longer eat beef, and follow nearly all the Hindu patterns of marriage and festivals. They refuse to interdine with Koyas and deny that intermarriage between themselves and Koyas is permissible.

The language and culture of the Gommu Koyas has been influenced to a great extent by contact with Telugus. The same is true for Lingu and Bāsa Koyas. The former are reported to be Lingayats (Prasad, 1950:163-164). Little is known about Guṭṭa and Dōrla Koyas, but they are distinguished from Gommu Koyas by the fact that they have been less influenced by Hindu customs and still practice swidden agriculture. They also retain more of the cycle of agricultural rituals associated with swidden agriculture. Gommu Koyas regard Guṭṭa Koyas as being "wilder" and less "civilized," whereas Guṭṭa Koyas look down on the Gommu Koyas as an inferior group of brawlers and cattle thieves.[2]

To some extent these distinctions correlate with dialect differences. Gommu Koya, Lingu Koya, and Bāsa Koya have a higher percentage of Telugu loan words than either Guṭṭa or Dōrla Koya. In Guṭṭa, Gommu, and Bāsa Koya there is a regular transition in the glottalized allophones of /h/ from Guṭṭa *[ʔ]*, Gommu *[ʼ]* ~ *[h]* to Bāsa *[ϕ]*. Lingu Koya probably aggrees with Bāsa Koya in this respect. Among those Gommu Koyas in frequent contact with Telugu speakers there is a tendency for *[h]* to disappear.

---

[2] For more complete ethnographic data, see Tyler, 1964.

Example:	Guṭṭa	[toˀt-]	'to bind, tie'
	Gommu	[toht-] ~ [tot-]	
	Bāsa	[tot-]	

Cf. Burrow and Bhattacharya, 1960:77.

A further feature is the appearance of an intrusive /s/ as a free variant of /ϕ/ in initial position in Gommu and Bāsa Koya. It occurs almost exclusively in lineage names shared by Koyas and Telugus.

Example: soyam oyam
sunnam undam
sōdi ōdi
sāriyam āriyam

Since all Telugu forms have initial /s/, Telugu is the source of this innovation. It does not represent a sporadic retention of original Gondi */s/ (cf. Burrow and Bhattacharya).

Of less certainty is the isogloss ṛ/ḍ between Guṭṭa and Gommu Koya. In general, Guṭṭa Koya has /ṛ/ where Gommu Koya has /ḍ/. This is particularly apparent in derivative suffixes, but appears to be less systematic in verb and noun bases.

Example:	Guṭṭa	mayyāṛi	'daughter'
	Gommu	mayyāḍi	

The Koya of Burrow and Bhattacharya (p. 75) on the other hand, seems to show /ṛ/ rather than /ḍ/ systematically.

On the basis of this rather sketchy evidence, Gommu and Bāsa (and probably Lingu) Koya should be classed as a single dialect differentiated from Guṭṭa Koya. The latter is probably nearer Dōrla Koya and the Koya of Malkanagiri. In general then, there are probably two dialects—a northern and a southern, but much field work remains to be done, especially with the northern dialects and Lingu Koya. This statement on dialects must remain purely provisional until further field data are available. Finally, it should be made explicit that this grammar represents only the Gommu dialect.

Chapter II

PHONOLOGY

2.1. Phonemics. There are twenty-nine segmental phonemes and eight suprasegmental phonemes.

2.2. Segmental phonemes. The segmental phonemes comprise ten vowel phonemes and nineteen consonant phonemes.

Vowels

	Front	Central	Back
High	i, ī		u, ū
Mid	e, ē		o, ō
Low		a, ā	

Consonants

	Bilabial	Dental	Dental-alveolar	Alveolar	Alveo-palatal	Pre-palatal cacuminical	Palatal	Velar	Post-velar
Stop	p b	t d				ṭ ḍ		k g	
Spirant			s						
Aspirate									h
Affricate					c j				
Flap				r					
Lateral			l						
Nasal	m		n			ṇ			
Fricative	v						y		

2.3. Distribution and allophony. Long vowels do not occur before geminate consonants. Front vowels occur utterance-initially with an on-glide [y]. Back vowels occur utterance-initially with an on-glide [v].

2.4. Vowels.

/a/

[ʌ̓] / C ___ # //
[a] / (C) ___ y //
[ạ] / (C) ___ {C̣, r} //
[ä] / (C) ___ m
  (C) ___ k(k)
  # ___ C_iC_j ($C_iC_j \rightarrow$ m, n, v, i = j)
  y ___ C(C) //
[ə] / else /

Distribution: initially, medially, finally.

Examples:	[ʌ̓]	ədzʌ́	'footprint'
		mǣ̣kʌ́	'goat'
		mɛṭ'ṭʌ'	'hill'
	[a]	ay'yo'	'not'
		pay'yʌ'	'after'
	[ạ]	mạr̃ri'	'son'
		ạḍ'ḍäm̃	'obstacle'
		ạr̃ri'	'path'
	[ä]	čäkřəβāti'	'emperor'
		äm̃mʌ'	'father's mother'
	[ə]	əd'dʉ	'it, she'

Description:	[ʌ̓]	a low, backed, tense vowel, stopped with a near glottal check.
	[a]	a mid, raised, tense allophone.
	[ạ]	a lax, retroflexed allophone.
	[ä]	a raised, fronted, tense allophone.
	[ə]	a lax, central, fronted allophone.

Contrasts:	mạṭ'ṭʌ'	'lineage name'
	mɛṭ'ṭʌ'	'mountain'
	mäk'kʌ'	'vagina'
	mʊk'kʌ'	'piece'
	bạr̃rʌ'	'spot'
	bạr̃re'	'donkey'
	əg'gẹ'	'there'
	ɪg'ge'	'here'
	vạr̃ri'	'paddy'
	vɛr̃ri'	'crazy'
	əläkäm̃	'displeasure'
	ɛläkʌ'	'permanent cultivation'
	ussi'	'having pounded'
	əssi'	'having bought'
	ɛssi'	'having shot'

nạ̄řʉ	'village'
nạ̄řʌ'	'twine'
mäk'kʌ'	'vagina'
mɑk'kʌ'	'maize'

/ā/

[ạ̄]	/ + { C̣ , r } //
[ā̈]	/ + y , y__C //
[ɔ̄̈]	/ + Cu# //
[ā]	/ else //

Distribution: initially, medially, finally.

Examples:	[ạ̄]	pạ̄ḍʌ'	'sing (imperative)'
		ạ̄ṭʌ'	'play (imperative)'
	[ā̈]	pā̈y'	'high, above'
		ā̈yit̲ānʌ'	'I will become'
		yā̈bā̈y	'fifty'
	[ɔ̄̈]	pɔ̄̈lʉ	'milk'
		ɔ̄̈lʉ	'wife'
		ɔ̄̈p̲ʉ	'stop' (transitive)
	[ā]	āg̲i'	'having stopped (intransitive)'
		āk̲e'	'that way'
		ālā	'in that way'
Description:	[ạ̄]	a lax, retroflexed allophone.	
	[ā̈]	a raised, tense allophone.	
	[ɔ̄̈]	a lower, backed, lax allophone.	
	[ā]	a mid-central, lax allophone.	
Contrasts:		pɔ̄̈lʉ	'milk'
		pōlʉ	'rice powder'
		ạṇḍʌ'	'protection, cover'
		ạ̄ṇḍʌ'	'female'
		ạ̄řʉ	'six'
		ēřʉ	'water'
		kɔ̄̈řʉ	'car'
		kōřʉ	'tusk'
		ạ̄ṭʌ'	'play (imperative)'
		ʊ̄ṭʌ'	'a kind of medicine'
		āk̲e'	'that way'
		īke'	'this way'

/i/

[ɪ]	/ + CC + C# + Ci + Ca	//
[iʼ]	/ C__#	//
[ị]	/ + Ç(Ç)	//
[i]	/ else	//

Distribution: initially, medially, finally.

Examples:	[ɪ]	ɪgʼgeʼ	'here'
		ɪdʼdʉ	'this'
		pɪɫlʌʼ	'child'
	[iʼ]	pəɦdiʼ	'pig'
		vīsiʼ	'fly'
	[ị]	pịṭʼṭeʼ	'bird'
		bịḍʼḍʌʼ	'female child'
	[i]	iřuvūřʉ	'both'
		mɪřiyāḵiʼ	'black pepper'

Description:	[ɪ]	a lax, backed, and somewhat lowered allophone.
	[iʼ]	a tense, checked allophone.
	[ị]	a lax, retroflexed allophone.
	[i]	a tense, front allophone.

Contrasts:	nịṇḍʌʼ	'shade'
	nīṇḍʌʼ	'full'
	dɪbʼbʌʼ	'heap, cover'
	dɛbʼbʌʼ	'beat'
	gəjʼjeʼ	'powerful'
	gəjʼjiʼ	'the itch'

/ī/

[ị̄]	/ + Ç	//
[ī]	/ else	//

Distribution: initially, medially, finally. Rare in final position.

Examples:	[ị̄]	ị̄ṭeʼ	'spear'
		bị̄ḍʉ	'wasteland'
	[ī]	pīḵɪḏiʼ	'female child'
		vīsiʼ	'fly'
		īḵeʼ	'this way'
		īlā	'in this way'

Description:	[ị̄]	a somewhat lax, retroflexed allophone.
	[ī]	a tense, high, front allophone.

Contrasts:

vīlʉ	'consent'
vēlʉ	'finger'
mīk̲ʉ	'to, for you'
mēk̲ʉ	'nail'

/e/

[ɛ] / + Ci
+ CC
+ C#
+ Ca //

[eʼ] /C__# //
[e] / else //

Distribution: initially, medially, finally.

Examples:

[ɛ]	mɛṭʼṭʌʼ	'mountain'
	bɛskeʼ	'when'
[eʼ]	bɛgʼgeʼ	'where'
	ɛḍʼḍiʼ	'sunshine'
[e]	eḍʉ	'front'
	elʉ	'rat'

Description:

[ɛ] a lax, somewhat lowered and retracted allophone.
[eʼ] a higher-mid, tense allophone stopped with a slight glottal check.
[e] a mid-front, tense allophone.

Contrasts:

nɛlʌʼ	'moon'
nǣlʌʼ	'earth'
eḍʉ	'front'
ēḍʉ	'seven'
pɛṭʼṭeʼ	'box'
piṭʼṭeʼ	'bird'
āk̲eʼ	'that way'
āk̲iʼ	'leaf'
mɛṭʼṭʌʼ	'mountain'
maṭʼṭʌʼ	'lineage name'

/ē/

[ǣ] / + C{a, o} // (in initial syllables only)
[ē] / else //

Distribution: initially, medially, finally. Rare finally except as an intensive suffix.

Examples: [ǣ] tǣg̱ʌ' 'clan'
lǣŋgʌ' 'calf'
tǣđ̱ʌ' 'difference'

[ē] ēṭe' 'crayfish'
ēmuɫ 'tortoise'
tēḏi' 'date'

Description: [ǣ] a lowered, retracted allophone.
[ē] a mid-front, tense allophone.

Contrasts: pēŋkʉ 'gods'
pɛ̄ŋkʉ 'tiles'

ēṭe' 'crayfish'
ī̤ṭe' 'spear'

ēřʉ 'water'
ạ̄řʉ 'six'

/u/

[ʉ] / C—# //
[u] / else //

Distribution: initially, medially, finally.

Examples: [ʉ] ǟββʉ 'they (feminine neuter)'
ọ̄ṇḍʉ 'he'

[u] duββʉ 'tiger'
uspāli' 'pestle'

Description: [ʉ] a tense, fronted unrounded allophone.
[u] a high, back, slightly rounded allophone.

Contrasts: uḍ- 'to plow'
ūḍ- 'to see'

məɫlʉ 'peacock'
məɫli' 'girl's name'

bug'gʌ' 'cheek'
bog'gʉ 'charcoal'

mēḵʉ 'nail'
mǣḵʌ' 'goat'

/ū/

[ʊ̄]	/ + Ca //	(except d͜z)
[ū]	/ else //	

Distribution: initially, medially. Rare after /l/.

Examples:	[ʊ̄]	pʊ̄sä̃m̃	'lineage name'
		kʊ̄řʌ́	'curry'
	[ū]	pūŋgạ̄ři'	'flower'
		gūn̲ji	'post'
Description:	[ʊ̄]	a tense, fronted, somewhat lowered back vowel.	
	[ū]	a high, back, slightly rounded allophone.	
Contrasts:		ūḍ-	'to see'
		uḍ-	'to plow'
		kʊ̄řʌ́	'curry'
		kōřʉ	'tusk'
		mʊ̄lʌ́	'corner'
		mālʌ́	'a Hindu caste'
		ʊ̄ṭʌ́	'a medicine'
		ā̤ṭʌ́	'play (imperative)'

/o/

[oʼ]	/ C__# //	
[ȫ]	/ + C_i $(C)_j$ //	(C (C) → y, v, n), (i = j)
[ɷ]	/ + Ca // / + k(k) //	(restricted to initial syllables)
[ọ]	/ + Ç //	
[o]	/ else //	

Distribution: initially, medially, finally.

Examples:	[oʼ]	tāt̲oʼ	'mother's father'
		dād̲oʼ	'father's father'
	[ȫ]	mȫyyɛɫ	'cloud'
		ȫββōři'	'salt'
	[ɷ]	dɷkʼkʌ'	'stomach'
	[ọ]	pọḍud̲ʉ	'morning'
	[o]	kot̲i'	'monkey'
		molōli'	'hare'
Description:	[oʼ]	a mid-back vowel stopped with a slight glottal check.	
	[ȫ]	a tense, unrounded, slightly raised allophone.	

	[ɒ]	a lax, lowered, retracted allophone
	[ọ]	a retroflexed allophone
	[o]	a low, back, unrounded allophone.

Contrasts:

mɒk̉kʌ̉	'maize'
mʊk̉kʌ̉	'piece'
kāk̲i̓	'crow'
kāk̲ȯ	'mother's mother'
mɒk̉kʌ̉	'maize'
mäk̉k̉ʌ̓	'vagina'
bog̉gʉ	'charcoal'
bug̉gʌ̉	'cheek'

/ō/

[ō̈]	/ + y //
[ɒ̄]	/ + Ça //
[ọ̄]	/ + Ç //
[ō]	/ else //

Distribution: initially, medially, finally. Rare finally except as a dubitative suffix.

Examples:

[ō̈]	ō̈yi̓	'porcupine'
	pō̈ye̓	'father's sister'
[ɒ̄]	tɒ̄ḍʌ̉	'thigh'
	dɒ̄ḍʌ̉	'boiled rice'
[ọ̄]	tọ̄ḍe̓	'wolf'
	vǣsọ̄ḍi̓	'tale'
[ō]	ōr̆ʉ	'they, masculine'
	yōg̲i̓	'ascetic'

Description: Allophones as for /o/ except for length.

Contrasts:

ōr̆ʉ	'they, masculine'
ạ̄r̆ʉ	'six'
ōr̆ʉ	'they, masculine'
ēr̆ʉ	'water
ōr̆ʉ	'they, masculine'
īr̆ʉ	'they, masculine proximate'
ọ̄ḍ-	'to lose at play'
ūḍ-	'to see'

2.5. Consonants.

/p/

[p̱]	/ V̄__V //
[p']	/ + p //
[p]	/ else //

Distribution: initially, medially.

Examples:	[p̱]	tɔ̃p̱äḵä̈y'	'to appear'
		pāp̱ä̃m̃	'sin, pity'
	[p']	əp'pʉ	'loan'
		təp'pʉ	'mistake'
		təp'pe'	'father'
	[p]	pɛd'dēři'	'name'
		pǣḵʌ'	'boy'
		pịṭʌ'	'stool'
		pịṭ'ṭe'	'bird'
		pūd͜zʌ'	'worship'

Description:	[p̱]	a lax, voiceless bilabial stop, formed without aspiration.
	[p']	a tense, voiceless, unreleased bilabial stop.
	[p]	a tense, voiceless, bilabial stop, formed without aspiration.

Contrasts:	pǣḏʌ'	'manure'
	bǣḏʌ'	'one-fourth anna'
	paṇḍi'	'fruit'
	baṇḍi'	'cart'
	təp'pɪs	'to avoid (causative)'
	təb'bɪs	'kind of hemp'
	pəṉče'	'dhoti'
	məṉče'	'field platform'
	mɪt͜sʌ'	'scorpion'
	pɪt͜sʌ'	'fart'
	əββʉ	'they (feminine neuter)'
	əp'pʉ	'loan'

/b/

[bʷ]	/ #__ɔ̃ //
[b']	/ + b //
[ƀ]	/ V__V //
[b]	/ else //

Distribution: initially, medially. Rare intervocalically.

Examples: [bʷ] bʷʊ̄d̠ʌ̓ 'understanding'

[b̓] əb̓bo̓ 'alas'
təb̓bɪs 'kind of hemp'

[ƀ] bɔ̤̄ƀʉ 'sir'

[b] bā̤ṭo̓ 'elder male cross-cousin'
bēnō̤ṇḍʉ 'who'

Description: [bʷ] a voiced bilabial stop produced with lip rounding and slight friction.

[b̓] an unreleased, tense voiced bilabial stop.

[ƀ] a lax, voiced bilabial stop.

[b] a tense, voiced bilabial stop.

Contrasts:
bǣd̠ʌ̓ 'one-fourth anna'
pǣd̠ʌ̓ 'manure'

bāt̠ʌ̓ 'what'
pāt̠ʌ̓ 'old'

ub̓bu- 'to swell'
um̃mu- 'to burn'

bəɫlʌ̓ 'table'
βəɫlʌ̓ 'net'

/t/

[t̠] / V__V //
[t̓] / + C //
[t] / else //

Distribution: initially, medially.

Examples: [t̠] tāt̠o̓ 'mother's father'
tāt̠i̓ 'lineage name'

[t̓] mɛt̓tʌ̓ 'mountain'

[t] tēk̠ʉ 'teak'
tā̤ḍʉ 'rope'
tīg̠e̓ 'creeper'

Description: [t̠] a lax, voiceless dental stop articulated as [t] but with slight friction.

[t̓] as [t] except unreleased.

[t] a tense, voiceless dental stop articulated with the blade of the tongue placed against the back of the upper teeth.

Contrasts:
pā̤ṭʌ̓ 'song'
pāt̠ʌ̓ 'old'

pəṯi'	'every'
pəḏi'	'ten'
čɪnnʌ'	'small'
tɪnnäk̲ǟy'	'right hand'
ts̆ɔ̈̄lᵘ	'furrow'
tɔ̈̄lʉ	'husk
dāḏo'	'father's father'
tāṯo'	'mother's father'

/ṭ/

[ṭ'] / + C //
[ṭ] / else //

Distribution: medially and initially in loan words.

Examples:	[ṭ']	pɛṭ'ṭi'	'small bank or dam'
		pɛṭ'ṭe'	'box'
		piṭ'ṭe'	'bird'
	[ṭ]	bāṭo'	'elder male cross-cousin'
		pāṭēḏi'	'bard'
		pīṭʌ'	'stool'
		ts̆āṭi'	'secret'
		ṭōp̲i'	'hat'
		ṭǟym̃	'time'

Description: [ṭ'] an unreleased, somewhat lax, unvoiced, post-alveolar stop.

[ṭ] tense, unvoiced, unaspirated post-alveolar (pre-palatal cacuminical) stop.

Contrasts:	bāṯo'	'whatever'
	pāṯʌ'	'old (thing)'
	bāṭo'	'elder male cross-cousin'
	pāṭʌ'	'song'
	kʷɔ̄̃ḍʌ'	'hatred'
	kʷɔ̄̃ṭʌ'	'fort'

/d/

[ḏ] /V__V//
[d'] / + C//
[d] / else //

Distribution: initially, medially, finally.

Examples:	[d̲]	dād̲o'	'father's father'
		bǣd̲ʌ'	'one-fourth anna'
		ād̲i'	'first'
	[d']	lod'di'	'valley'
		pəd'di'	'pig'
	[d]	pəšɛd	'personal name'
		dīƀe'	'excessive'
		dɔ̃ḍʌ'	'cooked rice'

Description:	[d̲]	a lax, voiced dental stop articulated like [t̲].
	[d']	a lax, voiced dental stop articulated like [t], but unreleased.
	[d]	a tense, voiced dental stop articulated like [t] except for voicing.

Contrasts:	dɛb'bʌ'	'a blow'
	ḍəb'bʉ	'money'
	dāβuḍʌ'	'cheek'
	tāβuḍʉ	'inner husk of rice'
	gaḍ'ḍe'	'throne'
	gaṭ'ṭi'	'hard'

/ḍ/

[ḍ'] / + C //
[ḍ] / else //

Distribution: initially, medially, finally. Rare both initially and finally.[1]

Examples:	[ḍ']	gaḍ'ḍe'	'throne'
	[ḍ]	ḍǣgʌ'	'hawk'
		ḍām̃ūr̆i'	'vulture'
		āḍʌ'	'to play'
		aḍɪβi'	'forest'
		ēḍʉ	'seven'
		uḍ'ḍ-	'to turn about'
		ūḍ-	'to see'
		tɔ̃ḍʌ'	'thigh'
		tōḍe'	'wolf'
		mūlāk̲əpāḍ	'village name'
		sɛk̲aṇḍ	'second'
		gr̆ēḍ	'grade'

[1] ṭ, ḍ, ṇ are not true retroflexes. The tip of the tongue is extended to the roof of the mouth, but it is not curled back as it would be for retroflexion. I have described these as post-alveolar, or as pre-palatal cacuminical, but otherwise will refer to them as retroflex in accordance with accepted usage.

Description:	[ḍ’]	an unreleased, voiced, unaspirated post-alveolar stop.
	[ḍ]	a tense, voiced, unaspirated post-alveolar stop.

Contrasts:

ạḍ’ḍäm̃	'obstacle'
əd’däm̃	'mirror'
kạ̄ḍʉ	'burial ground'
kạ̄ṭʉ	'a bite, a notch'
ḍǣg̲ʌ’	'hawk'
tǣg̲ʌ’	'clan'
tΩ̄ḍʌ’	'thigh'
tΩ̄ṭʌ’	'garden'

/k/

[kʷ] / + Ω̄ //
[k̲] / V__V ; h + //
[k’] / + C //
[k] / else //

Distribution: initially, medially.

Examples:	[kʷ]	kʷΩ̄hlʌ’	'millet'
		kʷΩ̄ḍʌ’	'hatred'
		kʷΩ̣̄ṇḍʌ’	'ox'
	[k̲]	pōhk̲ʉ	'guts'
		kāk̲o’	'mother's mother'
		kīk̲e’	'fish'
	[k’]	äk’kʌ’	'elder sister'
	[k]	kʊ̄ř̌ʌ’	'curry'
		kăk’ṭọṇḍʉ	'he vomited'

Description:	[kʷ]	a voiceless velar stop with labialized release. The back of the tongue is raised against the velum in a more forward position than for [k].
	[k̲]	a lax, unaspirated voiceless velar stop. Articulation is the same as for [k].
	[k’]	the same as [k] except unreleased.
	[k]	a tense, unaspirated voiceless velar stop. The back of the tongue is raised against the velum.

Contrasts:

mǣg̲ʌ’	'cloud'
mǣk̲ʌ’	'goat'
gʷΩ̄ḍʌ’	'wall'
kʷΩ̄ḍʌ’	'hatred'

/g/

[gʷ]	/ + Ω̄ //
[g']	/ + C //
[g̱]	/ V__V //
[g]	/ else //

Distribution: initially, medially.

Examples:	[gʷ]	vēŋgʷΩ̄lä m̃	'panther'
		gʷΩ̄ḍʌ'	'wall'
	[g']	gog'gi'	'unfilled ear of maize'
	[g̱]	pΩ̄g̱ǟy'	'tobacco'
		nəg̱ʌ'	'jewel'
	[g]	gāli'	'wind'
		g̣ạḍ'ḍe'	'throne'
		g̣ạḍ'ḍi'	'grass'

Description:	[gʷ]	a voiced velar stop with labialized release. Articulated like [kʷ] except for voicing.
	[g']	a lax, voiced, unaspirated, unreleased velar stop.
	[g̱]	a lax, voiced, unaspirated velar stop. Articulated like [g], but with slightly more friction.
	[g]	a tense, voiced, unaspirated velar stop. Articulated like [k] except for voicing.

Contrasts:	gäm̱pʌ'	'large basket'
	käm̱pʌ'	'thorn'
	əg'ge'	'there'
	äk'kʌ'	'elder sister'
	mäk'kʌ'	'female sex organ'
	məg'gä m̃	'loom'

/s/

[ś]	/ + ǣ //
[š]	/ + / ī̑ / //
	/ + / ē̑ / //
[ṣ̌]	/ + ṭ //
[s]	/ else //

Distribution: initially, medially, finally.

Examples:	[ś]	śǣnʌ'	'much'
		śǣḵʌ'	'branch'
	[š]	šɪβä m̃	'shake'
		pəšɛd	'proper name'
		pəši'	'young'

	[ṣ̌]	nɒṣ̌ṭʌʼ	'forehead'
		kạṣ̌ṭām̃	'difficulty'
	[s]	pǖsām̃	'lineage name'
		pusteʼ	'marriage necklace'
		som̃mʉ	'wages'
		sən̲čiʼ	'bag'
		təbʼbɪs	'kind of hemp'
		vīs	'dry measurement'

Description: [ś] a tense, voiceless dento-alveolar spirant, articulated with the tip of the tongue against the back of the lower teeth, and with the back of the tongue raised against the alveolus.

[š] a voiceless, palatalized alveolar spirant.[2]

[ṣ̌] a voiceless, post-alveolar spirant.

[s] a voiceless, dento-alveolar blade-slit spirant.

Contrasts:	sutʼtiʼ	'hammer'
	t͡sutʼtʉ	'around'
	sīleʼ	'piece of cloth'
	čīřeʼ	'sari'
	sālʌʼ	'stable'
	t͡sālʌʼ	'much'

/h/

[h] / + C //

[ɦ] / else //

Distribution: initially, medially. Does not occur in gemination.

Examples:	[h]	pōhkʉ	'guts'
		toht-	'bind'
	[ɦ]	ɦāni	'injury'
		ɦədʼdʉ	'order'
		ɦākʼkiʼ	'mortar'
		sələɦʌʼ	'advice'
		ɛɦeʼ	'exclamation—look out, go away'

Description: [h] a voiceless, post-velar aspirate. Varies freely with [ʼ], a slight glottal check.

[ɦ] a voiced post-velar aspirate.

[2] [š] is a free variant of [č] initially before [ɪ], [ī], [e], [ɛ], [ē].

Examples:	čēnʉ ~ šēnʉ	'field'
	čɪnnʌʼ ~ šɪnnʌʼ	'small'

Contrasts:	ɦāni'	'injury'
	sāni'	'lord'
	ɦäk'ki'	'mortar'
	käk'ki'	'having vomited'

/c/

[t͜s] / + back vowels (except ä) // + m // + t // + k //

[č] / else //

Distribution: initially, medially. Does not occur singly intervocalically, except after a long vowel. There is free variation between VččV and V̄čV, e.g., būči, bučči.

Examples:	[t͜s]	lət͜smay'ya	'personal name'
		būt͜say'ya	'personal name'
		t͜sāp̱ʌ'	'mat'
		t͜sɔ̄̈βʉ	'death'
		t͜soɫte'	'go-between'
		t͜sut'tʉ	'around'
		kạřt͜sʉ	'expense'
	[č]	tohči	'having bound'
		mənče'	'field platform'
		ləčči	'personal name'
		būči	'personal name'
		čäm̃ạtʌ'	'sweat'
		čämpʌ'	'cheek'
		čäkřəβāṯi'	'emperor'

Description: [t͜s] a lax, voiceless alveo-palatal affricate. The plosive component is a blade alveolar [ṯ]. The released component is a dento-alveolar blade-slit spirant [s].

[č] a tense, voiceless palatalized alveolar affricate. In gemination, the initial component is a blade alveolar [ṯ], the second component is [č].[3]

[3][č] has free variants [š] before front vowels except ä and [k͜s], or [t͜č] medially before /m/ and [ä].

Examples:	lət͜čämmʌ' ~ lək͜šäm̃mʌ'	'personal name'
	čĩm̃ʉ ~ šĩm̃ʉ	'mucus'
	čēnʉ ~ šēnʉ	'field'
	čɪŋgʉ ~ šɪŋgʉ	'edge, border of material'
	sāk͜ṣe' ~ sāt͜če' ~ sāče'	'witness'

Contrasts:	čǣḏʌ'	'bucket'
	ǰǣḍʌ'	'plait of hair'
	būǰi'	'feminine personal name'
	būči'	'feminine personal name'
	čīře'	'sari'
	sīle'	'piece of cloth'

/j/

[d͜z]	/ + back vowels //
[ᵈ͜s]	/ n__t //
[ǰ]	/ else //

Distribution: initially, medially. Does not occur singly intervocalically except after a long vowel. There is free variation between Vǰǰ V and V̄ǰV, e.g., būǰi', buǰǰi'.

Examples:	[d͜z]	əd͜zʌ'	'footprint'
		d͜zūn	'June'
		d͜zām̃	'kind of fruit'
		nɪd͜zǟm̃	'true'
		d͜zāβʌ'	'gruel'
	[ᵈ͜s]	kēnᵈ͜sṭōṇḍʉ	'he heard'
		gunᵈ͜sṭōṇḍʉ	'he wrestled'
		unᵈ͜sṭōṇḍʉ	'he slept'
	[ǰ]	ǰēli'	'delay'
		ǰīβʌ'	'life'
		ǰīṯǟm̃	'wage'

Description:

[d͜z] a lax, voiced alveo-palatal affricate. The first component is an unreleased back alveolar [ḍ] formed by placing the blade of the tongue against the rear portion of the alveolar ridge. It is released by formation of a voiced palatalized alveolar spirant.

[ᵈ͜s] The plosive component is a lightly voiced, unreleased central alveolar [ḏ'] formed by placing the front of the blade in the center of the alveolus. The second component is a dento-alveolar blade-slit spirant, formed with the foreblade of the tongue placed at the juncture of the teeth and the alveolus. The tongue has a slight groove in the center.

[ǰ] a tense, voiced alveo-palatal affricate. In gemination, the initial plosive component is a voiced, unreleased central alveolar [ḏ'] formed as for [ᵈ͜s].

Contrasts:	čǣḏʌ'	'bucket'
	ǰǣḍʌ'	'plait of hair'

būǰi'	'feminine personal name'
būči'	'feminine personal name'
əd͜zʌ'	'footprint'
ət͜sʌ'	'pure, clear'

/r/

[r̃] / + dental stops // + r //

[ř] / else //

Distribution: initially, medially, finally. Rare finally.

Examples:	[r̃]	pɪr̃ti'	'affection'
		pur̃ti'	'complete'
		ạr̃de'	'in path'
	[ř]	ạřʌ'	'half'
		pɛřke'	'after, behind'
		řɛṇḍʉ	'two'
		řād͜zʉ	'king'
		řōg̱äm̃	'disease'
		řup̱äy	'rupee'
		řɛk'kʌ'	'wing'
		poḏɛř	'weed'
		ḍäyβạř	'driver'
		nāβuḵạř	'servant'

Description:	[r̃]	a spirantized alveolar. In gemination r̃r is trilled with some spirantization.
	[ř]	a tense alveolar single flap.

Contrasts:	ạ̄řʌ'	'half'
	alʌ'	'wave'
	kəɫlʉ	'palmwine'
	kar̃rʉ	'plowshare'
	řɛk'kʌ'	'wing'
	lɛk'kʌ'	'account'
	ēřʉ	'water'
	ēḍʉ	'seven'
	kālʉ	'leg'
	kāřʉ	'car'
	kạ̄ḍʉ	'burial ground'
	řāni'	'queen'
	dāni'	'it, she (obj.)'
	řēše'	'lineage name'
	dēšäm̃	'country'

/l/

[ł̃]	/ + velar stops //
[ł]	/ + stops + h + l + # //
[l]	/ else //

Distribution: initially, medially, finally. Varies freely with ḷ. Rare initially before /u/ or /ū/.

Examples:	[ł̃]	pəł̃kʉ	'teeth'
		nāł̃keʼ	'tongue'
	[ł]	pāłdeʼ	'in milk'
		pɛłdeʼ	'in marriage'
		nułleʼ	'mosquito'
		kāłpʌʼ	'time, era'
		ɛłpʉ	'symbol of deity'
		pɛłliʼ	'marriage'
		kətʼtuł	'cot'
		mēńduł	'back'
		ēm̃uł	'tortoise'
		kɛt̠uł	'shed'
		gubʼbāł	'hillock'
	[l]	lən̠ǰeʼ	'prostitute'
		lɪŋgʉ	'lingam'
		lodʼdiʼ	'arrow'
		lēyọ̄ṇḍʉ	'young man'
		ōliʼ	'dowry'
		lɛkʼkʌʼ	'account, math'
		nɛlʌʼ	'moon, month'
		lōnʉ	'house'
		lāβʉ	'fat, large, great, excessive'

Description:	[ł̃]	a velarized lateral sonant with slight spirantization. The back of the tongue is raised toward the hard palate. The tongue tip is placed against the upper dentals and the blade against the alveolus.
	[ł]	a velarized lateral sonant. The back of the tongue is raised toward the hard palate.
	[l]	a dento-alveolar lateral sonant. The tongue blade is pressed against the alveolus and the tongue is spread.

Contrasts: see /r/

/m/

[m̃] / + m, + #, V_V //

[m̲] / + homorganic stop //

[m] / else //

Distribution: initially, medially, finally.

Examples:	[m̃]	ām̃mʌ’	'father's mother'
		däm̃mʉ	'time'
		īm̃ʉ	'give' (imperative)
		ēm̃uɫ	'tortoise'
		tām̃oʼ	'lineage name'
		pūnem̃	'lineage name'
		mạḍäk̲äm̃	'lineage name'
	[m̲]	əm̲bali’	'gruel'
	[m]	mạr̃ri’	'son'
		mǣg̲ʌ’	'cloud'

Description:	[m̃]	a lax bilabial sonant. The lips are stretched and make only slight contact.
	[m̲]	a homorganic nasal.
	[m]	a tense bilabial sonant. The lips are pressed tightly together, but not rounded.

Contrasts:	mäk’kʌ’	'vagina'
	näk’kʌ’	'jackal'
	päk’kʌ’	'beside'
	äm̃mʌ’	'father's mother'
	äββʌ’	'mother'
	ännʌ’	'elder brother'
	mǣd̲ʌ’	'two-story house'
	bǣd̲ʌ’	'one-fourth anna'
	βạ̄ṭʌ’-	'put' (imperative)
	mạ̄ṭʌ’	'word'

/n/

[n̲] / + č, + ǰ //

[ñ] / + ǣ, g + //

[ŋ] / + #, + velar stops //

[ń]	/ + dental stops //
[ṇ]	/ + Ç //
[n]	/ else //

Distribution: initially, medially, finally.

Examples:	[n̲]	ən̲ǰi'	'having gone'
		mɛn̲či'	'good'
	[ñ]	ñǣp̲äk̲äm	'memory'
		əgñāɫ	'command'
	[ŋ]	pūŋgạri'	'flower'
		pēŋkʉ	'gods'
		äm̃māŋ	'mothers'
		pȫyēŋ	'father's sisters'
		vīsīŋ	'flies'
	[ń]	tıńtānʌ'	'I will eat'
		əńde'	'anklet'
	[ṇ]	nị̄ṇḍʌ'	'shade'
		nạ̄ṇḍʉ	'day'
		ọ̄ṇḍʉ	'he'
		pạṇḍi'	'fruit'
	[n]	nənnʌ'	'I'
		nɛlʌ'	'moon'
		nǣlʌ'	'earth'
		nōm̃ʉ	'pain'

Description:	[n̲]	blade alveolar.
	[ñ]	palatal—in initial position varies freely with [n].
	[ŋ]	velar.
	[ń]	apical-dental.
	[ṇ]	a pre-palatal, cacuminical nasal resonant.
	[n]	a blade dento-alveolar.

Contrasts:	řāni'	'queen'
	řām̃i'	'feminine personal name'
	mā	'our,' 'my' (plural)
	nā	'my'
	ạṇḍʌ'	'cover'
	əńde'	'anklet'

/ṇ/

[ṇ]

Distribution: medially. Infrequently clusters with itself.

Examples: [ṇ] āṇeʼ 'younger male cross-relative of son's generation'

aṇā 'anna'

āṇəlōřʉ 'ancestors'

pāṇām̃ 'breath'

paṇṇīŋ 'fruits'

gāṇum̃ 'census'

kāṇiʼ 'one-sixteenth anna'

uṇ- 'to drink'

Description: a pre-palatal, cacuminical nasal resonant. The tongue-tip is pressed against the forepart of the hard palate, just behind the alveolar ridge. The tongue-tip is not reverted

Contrasts:

ā lānē 'in just that way'
āṇeʼ 'younger male cross-relative of son's generation'

āṇəlōřʉ 'ancestors'
ānəβāliʼ 'a mark, impression'

uṇji 'having drunk'
un̲ji 'having slept'

kaṇət̲ʌʼ 'the temple'
kənaṭām̃ 'to bring forth'
kənɪt̲iʼ 'lineage name'
kaṇɪt̲iʼ 'wen or tumor'

/v/

[β] / # + back vowels
+ v
V__V //

[v] / else //

Distribution: initially, medially, finally. Frequent initially as an on-glide before back vowels.

Examples: [β] řāβʉ 'personal name'

oββōřiʼ 'salt'

βānʌʼ 'rain'

šɪβām̃ 'shake'

ǰīβʌʼ 'life'

t͜sɔ̄̈βʉ 'death'

ɪββʉ 'these'

kanβʌʼ 'channel'

βōṇḍʉ 'he'

[v] vēřʉ 'root'

vɪd͜zʌʼ 'seed'

Description:	[β]	a lax, voiced bilabial continuant with slight friction. Lips are spread and loosely pressed together. Lips are slightly rounded before [a].	
	[v]	a tense, voiced labio-dental continuant produced without lip-rounding.	

Contrasts:

βā̤ṭ-	'to put'
pā̤ṭ-	'to sing'
βəṉji’	'rice'
məṉji’	'having been'
bǣlʌ’	'what'
vǣlʌ’	'time, day, period'
ä̃m̃mʉ	'sell'
ä̃ββʉ	'they, feminine neuter'

/y/

[y’] / + y // ; / + # //

[y] / else //

Distribution: initially, medially, finally. Rare initially except as on-glide before front vowels.

Examples:	[y’]	yā̤ββā̤y’	'fifty'
		pā̤y’	'above'
		pay’yʌ’	'afterwards'
		nā̤y’	'dog'
		kā̤y’	'hand'
		ay’yʌ’	'father'
	[y]	yōgi’	'sage'

Description:	[y’]	a tense, voiced, checked, palatal continuant. Has slightly more friction than [i].
	[y]	as above except unchecked.

2.6. The foregoing analysis is based on words taken in isolation. In the appropriate context vowels are subject to a "fronting" process sinilar to that described in 2.3. Word initial vowels (short or long) have an onset glide y or v when preceded by the vowels i, a, e, o (short or long) or the consonant y. (For explanation of the meaning of symbols // //, ( ), and upper case letters in the examples to follow, see 2.20).

$$\overleftrightarrow{V}_i \rightarrow {}^\wedge\overleftrightarrow{V}_i \;/\; \left\{\begin{array}{l}\overleftrightarrow{V}_j \\ y\end{array}\right. \#\_\_// \;;\; {}^\wedge \rightarrow \left\{\begin{array}{l}y \\ v\end{array}\right. \;;\; \overleftrightarrow{V}_j \rightarrow \left\{\begin{array}{l}\bar{ı} \\ \bar{a} \\ \bar{e} \\ \bar{o}\end{array}\right.$$

(^) is a cover symbol for phonetic y and v.

$${}^\wedge V_i \rightarrow yV_i \;/\; \left\{\begin{array}{l}\underline{y} \\ \bar{e}\end{array}\right. \#\_\_//$$

$${}^\wedge\left\{\begin{array}{l}\bar{a} \\ \bar{u}\end{array}\right. \rightarrow v\left\{\begin{array}{l}\bar{a} \\ \bar{u}\end{array}\right. \;/\; \bar{o}\;\#\_\_//$$

$${}^\wedge\left\{\begin{array}{l}\bar{a} \\ \bar{o} \\ \bar{e} \\ \bar{ı}\end{array}\right. \rightarrow y\left\{\begin{array}{l}\bar{a} \\ \bar{o} \\ \bar{e} \\ \bar{ı}\end{array}\right. \;/\; \bar{ı}\;\#\_\_//$$

$${}^\wedge\bar{u} \rightarrow v\bar{u} \quad /\; \bar{ı}\;\#\_\_//$$

$${}^\wedge\left\{\begin{array}{l}\bar{a} \\ \bar{e} \\ \bar{ı}\end{array}\right. \rightarrow y\left\{\begin{array}{l}\bar{a} \\ \bar{e} \\ \bar{ı}\end{array}\right. \;/\; \bar{a}\#\_\_//$$

$${}^\wedge\left\{\begin{array}{l}\bar{u} \\ \bar{o}\end{array}\right. \rightarrow v\left\{\begin{array}{l}\bar{u} \\ \bar{o}\end{array}\right. \;/\bar{a}\#\_\_//$$

Examples:

//mī # ^amma// — 'your (formal) father's mother'
[mīyämm̃ʌ']

//mā #^ēndāḍi// — 'My (our) younger female cross-cousin'
[māyēńḍā̤ḍi']

//nī #^odeli// — 'your (informal) hearth'
[nīyoḏeli']

//ā# ^īte// — 'that spear'
[āyīṯe']

//ī# ^ūṭa// — 'this medicinal mixture'
[īvṳ̄ṭa]

//mī# ^āṇe// — 'your (formal) sister's son'
[mīyā̤ṇe']

//ī# ^ōli// — 'this bride price'
[īyōli']

//ā #nāy #^ūḍ+TT+ANA// — 'I saw that dog'
(ā #nāy #^ūḍ+t+āna)
[ānā̈yyṳ̄ḍtānʌ']

//ira+vay# ^ayḍu// — 'twenty-five'
[iřavā̈yyā̈yḍʉ]

//āru-+vāy#^ēḍu// [ạřavā̈yyẹ̄ḍʉ]	'sixty-seven'
//kāko#^ēs+CI// (kāko#^ēs+i) [kāk̲ovēsi']	'mother's mother having swept'
//bāṭo#^ī+CI// (bāṭo#^ī+si) [bạ̄ṭovīsi']	'elder male cross-cousin having given'
//tāto#^ā+CI// (tāto#^ā+si) [tāt̲ovāsi']	'mother's father having become'
//dādo#^ūḍ+CI// (dādo#^ūḍ+i) [dād̲ovūḍi']	'father's father having seen'
//bāṭo#^ett+CI// (bāṭo#^ett+i) [bạ̄ṭovet'ti']	'elder male cross-cousin having lifted'
//kāko#^all+CI// (kāko#^all+i) [kāk̲ovałli']	'mother's mother having sprinkled'
//orro#^uspāli// [or̃ovuspāli']	'one pestle'
//mūṇḍō#^ungaram// [mụ̄ṇḍōvuŋgạřā̃m̃]	'third ring'
//mance#^ūḍ+CI// (mance#^ūḍ+i) [mən̲čeyụ̄ḍi']	'field platform having seen'
//binde#^ō+CI// (binde#^ō+si) [bıńdeyōsi']	'metal pot having brought'
//pinde#^ī+CI// (pinde#^ī+si) [pıńdeyīsi']	'fruit buds having given'
//pinde#^ā+CI// (pinde#^ā+si) [pıńdeyāsi']	'fruit buds having become'
//peṭṭe#^ett+CI// (peṭṭe#^ett+i) [pɛṭ'ṭeyet'ti']	'box having lifted'
//tappe#^ass+CI// (tappe#^ass+i) [təp'peyassi']	'father having sold'

//kappe# ^uḍḍ+CI// 'frog having returned'
(kappe# ^uḍḍ+i)
[kəp'peyuḍ'ḍi']

//ālā+nē# ^ūpiri// 'in just that way breath'
[ālānēyūpɪr̆i']

2.7. Suprasegmental Phonemes. The eight suprasegmental phonemes consist of five juncture phonemes and three pitch phonemes.

Juncture: The five juncture phonemes consist of one internal and four terminal junctures.

Internal	/+/
Terminal	/,/
	/./
	/:/
	/;/

2.8. The phonetic components of these phonemes are as follows:

[:]	prolongation of preceding phoneme.
[.]	slight prolongation of preceding phoneme.
[4]	extra high pitch.
[3]	high pitch.
[2]	middle pitch.
[1]	low pitch.

2.9. /+/ morpheme boundary. Characterized by a combination of [.] and [2]-[2].

Examples:

[²bū. ²či']	'feminine personal name'
[²kəɫ. ²lʉ]	'palm wine'
[²paṇ. ²ḍi']	'fruit'

/+/ thus differs from "closed" juncture characteristic of normal transition from one segmental phoneme to another.

2.10. /,/ Pause juncture is characterized by [:] and [2] - [2].
Example:
[²ag' gé mən̠ji: ²ɪg' ge' vət'tọṇḍʉ] 'having stayed there, he came here'

2.11. /:/ Pause juncture is characterized by [:] and [2] - [4], [3] - [2].

Examples:

[²kā⁴ni':]	'but'
[³kā²ni':]	'but'

/:/ may or may not occur before silence.

2.12. /;/ Period juncture is characterized by [:] and [2]-[3], [2]-[4].

Examples:

[²nɪdzä³m̃ẽ:]	'indeed true'
[²əb'⁴bō:]	'alas'
[²tuŋgiṯī³ř̄ā:]	'you will do?'

/:/ occurs in utterances denoting emphasis, doubt, and interrogation, and only before silence.

2.13. /./ Period juncture is characterized by [:] and [2] - [1].

Examples:

[²ət'tōṇḍu':¹]	'he became'

/./ occurs in utterances denoting simple statements, and only before silence.

2.14. Pitch. The three pitch phonemes are: /1/ low pitch, /2/ middle pitch, /3/ high pitch. [4], extra high pitch, varies freely with /3/ and denotes no change of meaning. When combined, these phonemes comprise the following intonational contours: /2 - 1/, /2 - 2/, /2 - 3/, /3 - 2/, /2 - 3 - 2/, /2 - 3 - 3/.

Examples:

[²añdōřuvət'tīřā:³]	'did everyone come?'
[²ōṇḍutɪt'tōṇḍu:¹]	'he ate'
[²řōgām̃ɪt'kᵘ;řōgä³m̃ē':]	'a disease is a disease'
[²nāḍi'.³bɛg'ge'²vət'tīři:]	'<u>where</u> did you go yesterday?'
[²nāḍi'³bātō'²tuŋgɪłe³nā:]	'isn't it true (you) did nothing yesterday?'
[²nī³maḍ'ḍʌ'³maṇḍʌ':]	'may your penis burn!'
[²kāβaṭ'ṭi':²]	'therefore'
[³kā²ni:]	'but'

2.15. Stress. There are two types of stress—strong and weak. Stress is predictable on the basis of juncture, syllable quantity, and pitch. Consequently, it is not phonemic.

In a phrase strong stress regularly occurs on the first syllable, each following syllable being more lightly stressed, but still distinguishable from weak stress. Within a word stress occurs with long syllables, i.e., (C)V̄, CVC, CV̄C, CV̄NC. Syllabic prominence occurs on vowels. Weak stress occurs with short syllables. In the examples that follow, weak stress is unmarked.

Examples:

pɪḱ'kʌ'	'calf of leg'
ā́ḵi'	'leaf'
pū́ŋgā́ři'	'flower'
tā́ṯo'	'mother's father'
kṓḍəβā́li'	'sickle'
gínne'	'cup'
kā́p̱uřām̃	'residence'
bɛ́ske'	'when'

ə́ndṓr̆ʉ	'everyone'
lə́n̲ǰe'	'prostitute'
vuy'yā́ɫ	'cradle'

Strong stress also occurs on the final syllable of a sequence before a terminal juncture when the intonation contour includes a falling pitch pattern.

Since stress is predictable it is not written in the subsequent material.

2.16. Syllable structure. The syllable canons are:

VC	əs-ke'
CV	pə-ti
CVC	mən̲-če'
CVCC	por̆l-tānʌ'
CVNC	tuŋg-tʌ'
CVCCC	pur̆sk-tʌ'
VCCC	er̆sk-tʌ'
V̄	ū-tʌ'
CV̄	lō-nʉ
CV̄C	nā̈y'
CV̄NC	nīŋg-tʌ'
[CCV]	vr̆ɪ-kṣ̌ām̃, təllām̲-br̆ʌ'

2.17. Words of up to six syllables may occur. CCV occurs initially only in unassimilated loan words deriving from Sanskrit or English, e.g., gr̆ēḍ 'grade'. (Final C must be a consonant phoneme capable of occurring in final position.)

2.18. Consonant clusters. Table 1 represents the occurrence of consonant clusters. With the exception of loan words noted above, consonant clusters do not occur initially or finally. An example of final clusters in loan words is sɛk̲aṇḍ.

The table includes two-consonant clusters, the first member of which can be a homorganic nasal. Other two-consonant clusters may be preceded by homorganic nasals.

Examples: mpt, ŋgt, ndt, njt, ntr, mbr, ṇḍt, ŋkt

Three-member clusters occur.

Examples: dkt, rsk, ptk, ctk, rtk, ktk, vtk, stk, djk, ltk; dkt is unusual.

Most three-member clusters have t as medial member followed by k. Where a voiced consonant might be expected in initial position, a vowel intervenes before t.

TABLE 1

Two-consonant Clusters

	p	b	t	d	ṭ	ḍ	k	g	s	h	c	j	r	l	m	n	ṇ	v	y
p	+		+	+									+					+	
b		+	+										+					+	
t			+	+					+		+		+	+		+		+	+
d			+	+							+	+	+	+		+		+	+
ṭ			+	+	+				+									+	
ḍ			+	+		+						+						+	
k			+				+		+				+						+
g			+					+								+			
s	+		+	+			+		+		+			+	+			+	
h			+				+											+	
c			+	+			+				+								
j				+			+					+							
r			+	+			+		+		+		+	+		+			
l	+		+	+			+						+	+	+	+		+	
m	+	+	+	+			+					+	+		+				+
n	+		+	+	+	+	+	+			+	+	+			+			+
ṇ			+	+	+	+					+	+					+		
v			+	+			+									+		+	
y			+	+			+		+							+		+	+

2.19. The preceding analysis is based on the occurrence of phonemes in words. Within phrases, many consonant sequences do not agree with the rules. The most convenient method is to consider that another type of juncture (#) occurs between words. This juncture is marked by the occurrence of primary stress on the first vowel following it.

2.20. Morphophonemic Rules and Cover Symbols. To facilitate analysis and presentation, cover symbols are used to express morphophonemic rules. These cover symbols are:

//\` //, //´ //, //@//, //ˇ //, // / //, //X//, //ɸ//, //&//

All morphophonemic writing is enclosed in // // with allomorphic cover symbols written in upper case letters. Utterances written with the appropriate morphemic variant rather than the cover symbol occur within ( ). Phonemic writing either occurs within / / or without identifying brackets. Unless otherwise specified these conventions apply throughout the remainder of the book.

2.21. // ` // describes one of the processes of vowel elision. Final short vowels are elided before initial vowels differing only in the component of length. Formulaically this is represented as follows:

$$V_i \rightarrow \bar{V}_j \ / \ \_\_\#\bar{V}_j// \quad (i = j)$$

The notation (i = j) indicates that the two vowels carrying the subscripts are equivalent.

Examples:

//orro` #ōṇḍu// 'one man'
/orrōṇḍu/

//lōnu + T + KI ` #īlā// 'to house in this way'
(lō + t + ki ` #īlā)
/lōtkīlā/

//ēnd + CORE ` #ēnd + CORE// 'dancing and dancing'
(ēnd + ōre ` #ēnd + ōre)
/ēndōrēndōre/

//lōnu + K ´ #anta ` #āvungu// 'to all houses meat'
(lō + hku ´#anta ` #āvungu)
/lōhkantāvungu/

2.22. // ´ // describes the second process of vowel elision. Final short a, i, u are elided before initial short or long vowels.

$$V_i \rightarrow \breve{\bar{V}}_j \ / \_\_ \left\{ \begin{matrix} \# \\ + \end{matrix} \breve{\bar{V}}_j \right. //, \quad V_i \rightarrow \left\{ \begin{matrix} a \\ i \\ u \end{matrix} \right.$$

Examples:

//pajja ´ #anta// 'all people'
/pajjanta/

//pulla ´ #ett + CI// 'stick having lifted"
(pulla ´ #ett + i)
/pulletti/

//ā #kuṇḍa ´ #orro// 'that pot one'
/ā kuṇḍorro/

//kōnga ´ #uḍḍ + CI// 'crane having turned about'
(kōnga ´ #uḍḍ + i)
/kōnguḍḍi/

//kōṇḍa ´ #inn + TT ϕ+KU// 'what is an oxen'
(kōṇḍa ´ #i + ttϕ+ku)
/kōṇḍitku/

//padi ´ #erra// 'ten red'
/paderra/

//nāru + T + NI ˊ#ōru ˊ#anta// 'whole village'
(nā + ṭē + ni ˊ#ōru ˊ#anta)
/nāṭēnōranta/

//tung + TT + A ˊ+ ōṇḍu// 'one (he) who did'
(tung + t + a ˊ+ ōṇḍu)
/tungtōṇḍu/

//tung + ANI& ˊ#ūgāy #paṇḍum// 'pickle festival doing'
(tung + āni& ˊ#ūgāy #paṇḍum)
/tunganūgāy paṇḍum/

//bāri ˊ#inn + TT + ONDU// 'why he said'
(bāri ˊ#i + tt + ōṇḍu)
/bārittōṇḍu/

//verkāḍi ˊ#ā + CI// 'having become a cat'
(verkāḍi ˊ#ā + si)
/verkāḍāsi/

//vīru ˊ #ira @ + URU// 'these both'
(vīru ˊ#ira @ + vūru)
/vīriruvūru/

//mūṇḍu ˊ #ēṇḍu + K// 'three years'
(mūṇḍu ˊ #ēṇḍu + ku)
/mūṇḍēṇḍku/

//kallu ˊ#ō X + TT + A #payya// 'palm wine which was brought'
(kallu ˊ#ō X + tt + a #payya)
/kallottapayya/

2.23. // ˇ // denotes a "fronting" process occurring with internal juncture. (cf. 2.3 and 2.6.) Suffix initial vowels (short or long) have an onset glide y or v when preceded by long vowels.

$$\overset{(-)}{V}_i \rightarrow {}^{\vee}\overset{(-)}{V}_i \;/\; \bar{V}_j + \_\_ /\!/; \quad {}^{\vee} \rightarrow \begin{Bmatrix} v \\ y \end{Bmatrix}$$

$${}^{\vee}i \rightarrow y\overset{(-)}{i} \;/\; \bar{V} + \_\_ /\!/$$

$${}^{\vee}\begin{Bmatrix} \bar{a} \\ \bar{o} \\ \bar{u} \\ \bar{e} \end{Bmatrix} \rightarrow y\begin{Bmatrix} \overset{(-)}{a} \\ \overset{(-)}{o} \\ \overset{(-)}{u} \\ \overset{(-)}{e} \end{Bmatrix} \;/\; \begin{Bmatrix} \bar{e} \\ \bar{a} \end{Bmatrix} + \_\_ /\!/$$

$${}^{\vee}\begin{Bmatrix} \bar{a} \\ \bar{o} \\ \bar{u} \\ \bar{e} \end{Bmatrix} \rightarrow v\begin{Bmatrix} \overset{(-)}{a} \\ \overset{(-)}{o} \\ \overset{(-)}{u} \\ \overset{(-)}{e} \end{Bmatrix} \;/\; \begin{Bmatrix} \bar{i} \\ \bar{o} \\ \bar{u} \end{Bmatrix} + \_\_ /\!/$$

$${}^{\vee}\bar{a} \rightarrow v\bar{a} \;/\; \bar{a} + \_\_ /\!/$$

Examples:

//ī + ˇIT + ONDU// 'he will give'
(ī + ˇit + ōṇḍu)
/īyitoṇḍu/

//vā + ˇIT + ONDU// 'he will come'
(vā + ˇit + ōṇḍu)
/vāyitōṇḍu/

//nā + KI / #kā + ˇāli// 'it is necessary to me'
(nā + ku / #kā + ˇāli)
/nākkāvāli/

//kē + ˇ it + ONDU// 'he will tell'
(kē + ˇ it + ōṇḍu)
/kēyitōṇḍu/

//ī + ˇ O + KU// 'if not give'
(ī + ˇū + ku)
/īvūku/

//kē + ˇO + KU// 'if not tell'
(kē + ˇ ū + ku)
/kēyūku/

//ā + ˇO + ˇA// 'not having become'
(ā + ˇo + ˇa)
/āyova/

2.24. //@// denotes vowel harmony with internal juncture. In unaccented syllables short i, u, a are changed to the vowel of the following syllable. When that vowel is i, u, or a (short or long) no change in vowel quantity occurs. This process is most common when the following vowel is long, but is not restricted to this environment.

$$\ldots CV_i(C) \rightarrow \ldots CV_j(C) \;/\; \_\_ + (C)\overset{(-)}{V}_j$$

$$V_i \rightarrow \begin{Bmatrix} i \\ u \\ a \end{Bmatrix} \qquad V_j \rightarrow \begin{Bmatrix} \bar{i} \\ \bar{u} \\ \bar{a} \end{Bmatrix}$$

Examples:

//ira@+vūru// 'both'
/iruvūru/

//vaṇa@k+IT+e// 'it will bend'
(vaṇa@k+īt+e)
/vaṇikīte/

//vāngu@+T+KI// 'to the river'
(vāngu@+t+ki)
/vāngitki/

//miga@l + IT + e// 'it will remain over'
(miga@l + īt + e)
/migilīte/

2.25. // / // denotes another process of vowel elision with word juncture. Final short a, i, u, are elided when preceded by a consonant equivalent (or equivalent except for retroflexion) to the initial consonant of the following word.

$$C_iV \rightarrow C_i \ / \ \_\#C_j// \qquad V \rightarrow \begin{Bmatrix} a \\ i \\ u \end{Bmatrix}$$

(i = j except in -tV#ṭ-, -ḍV#d-, -dV#ḍ, -ṭV#t)

Examples:

//nā + KI/#kā + ˇāli// 'to me it is necessary'
/nākkāvāli/

//pāta/#ṭōpi// 'old hat'
/pāttṭōpi/

//man + ANI/#nēṇḍu// 'day which is'
(mand + āni/#nēṇḍu)
/mandānnēṇḍu/

//āru/#rūpāy + K// 'six rupees'
(āru/#rūpāy + ku)
/ārrūpāyku/

//verkāḍi/#digg ϕ + TT + E// '(the) cat got down'
(verkāḍi/#digg ϕ + t + e)
/verkāḍdigte/

//bēnōru/#rēt + TT + A ˊ + agga// 'those who made vows there'
(bēnōru/#rē + t + a ˊ + agga)
/bēnōrrētagga/

//vāṇ + T + INNI/#namm + CI// 'having believed those'
(vāṇ + ṭ + īni/#namm + i)
/vāṇtīnnammi/

2.26. // X // denotes loss of vowel length with internal juncture when a final long vowel is followed by a geminated consonant.

$$\bar{V} \rightarrow V \ / \ \_ + C_iC_j // \qquad (i = j)$$

Examples:

//āX + TT + A + payya// 'after becoming'
(āX + tt + a + payya)
/attapayya/

//ōX + TT + ōṇḍu// 'he brought'
(ōX + tt + ōṇḍu)
/ottōṇḍu/

//kēX+ TT + ōṇḍu// 'he told'
(kēX + tt + ōṇḍu)
/kettōṇḍu/

//īX+ TT + ōṇḍu// 'he gave'
(īX + tt + ōṇḍu)
/ittōṇḍu/

2.27. // ϕ // denotes degemination with internal juncture when a geminated consonant is followed by another consonant.

$$C_iC_j \rightarrow C_iC_k \ / \ \_\_ + C_k \ // \quad (i = j)$$

Examples:

//āX+ TTϕ+ KU// 'if become'
(āX + ttϕ + ku)
/atku/

//ettϕ+ TT + ōṇḍu// 'he lifted'
(ettϕ + t + ōṇḍu)
/ettōṇḍu/

//diggϕ+ TT + ōṇḍu// 'he got down'
(diggϕ + t + ōṇḍu)
/digtōṇḍu/

//ussϕ+ TT + ōṇḍu// 'he ground'
(ussϕ + t + ōṇḍu)
/ustōṇḍu/

//nammϕ+ TT+ ANA// 'I believed'
(nammϕ + t + āna)
/namtāna/

2.28. // & // denotes a second process of loss of vowel length. It occurs when non-initial syllables or suffixes in V̄CV are followed by suffixes beginning in V̄ or VCC where CC is geminate.

$$\bar{V}CV \rightarrow VCV \ / \ \_\_ + \begin{Bmatrix} \bar{V} \\ VC_iC_j \end{Bmatrix} \ // \quad (i = j)$$

Examples:

//tung + ANI & ` + addu// 'which does'
(tung + āni & ` + addu)
/tunganaddu/

//tāt + āl & + ORU// 'mother's fathers'
(tāt + āl & + ōru)
/tātalōru/

2.29. Additional non-automatic morphophonemic rules are given in 3.58 and 4.8.

CHAPTER III

NOUNS, QUALIFIERS, AND MINOR FORM CLASSES

3.1. A noun (N) consists of a nucleus (base) plus or minus suffixes.

3.2. The nucleus is comprised either of a single, unanalyzable root morpheme, or of a root morpheme plus derivational suffixes. A noun nucleus may be monosyllabic or polysyllabic.

monosyllables:	nāy	'dog'
	kāy	'hand'
disyllables:	mallu	'peacock'
	balla	'table'
	tēku	'teak'
trisyllables:	ungaram	'ring'
	pātanam	'betrothal'
	vēngālam	'leopard'
four syllables:	kalektēru	'collector'

Monosyllabic nuclei are monomorphemic. Polysyllabic nuclei are analyzable into two or more morphemes—a root and formative suffixes. The first morpheme (root) is either unique or occurs in a limited number of nuclei. Only a few of the derivative suffixes may be assigned a meaning.

3.3. The canonical shapes of derivational suffixes are: V, C, CV, V̄C(V), VC(V), V̄NCV, VNCV, VCCV. The derivational suffixes consist of the following: -a, -e, -i, -u, -o, -m, -ūru, -āl, -āḍi, -uṇḍu, -ayya, -amma, -akka, -āri, -āli, -uru, -ava, -ḍa, -ḍi, -ta, -ti, -ke, -ka, -iki, -ku, -āyi, -ili, -iya, -ōli, -eli, -ūli, -īri, -ōri. All formative suffixes ending in -li or -yi are in free variation with allomorphs ending in -l or -y respectively.

3.4. -a. Nouns ending in -a constitute the largest single class. The plural is either /-ku/ or /-n/.

Examples:	amm-a	'mother's mother'
	ammān ~ ammāku	'mother's mothers'
	akk-a	'elder sister'
	akkān ~ akkāku	'elder sisters'
	mēk-a	'goat'
	mēkān ~ mēkāku	'goats'
	ar-a	'half'

3.5. -e. Nouns with the formative suffix -e form the plural with /-n/.

Examples:	āṇ-e	'sister's son'
	āṇēn	'sister's sons'
	īt-e	'spear'
	ītēn	'spears'
	piṭṭ-e	'bird'
	piṭṭēn	'birds'
	piṇḍ-e	'fruit bud'
	piṇḍēn	'fruit buds'
	kīk-e	'fish'
	kīkēn	'fish'

3.6. -o. Nouns with the formative suffix -o are rare, and all denote kinsmen or lineage names. The plural is /-ōru/ for males and /-ku/ ~ /-n/ for females. All -o ending kin terms for males have alternate formal formative suffixes in -āl.

Examples:	dād-o	'father's father'
	dādalōru	'father's fathers'
	tāt-o	'mother's father'
	tātalōru	'mother's fathers'
	bāṭ-o	'elder male cross-cousin'
	bāṭalōru	'elder male cross-cousins'
	kāk-o	'mother's mother'
	kākōku	'mother's mothers'

3.7. -i. Nouns with this suffix form the plural with /-n/. With personal names -i denotes females or a familiar form contrasting with the more formal suffixes -amma, -akka, -ayya, -āl.

Examples:	el-i	'rat'
	elīn	'rats
	pind-i	'flour'
	būc-i	'girl's name'
	rām-i	'girl's name'
	lacc-i	'girl's name'

3.8. -u. Nouns with -u comprise the second most frequently occurring class of nouns. They form the plural with /-ku/ or /-k/.

Examples:	tāḍ-u	'rope'
	tāḍuk	'ropes'
	tōng-u	'curd'
	tōnguk	'curds'

mall-u	'peacock'
malku	'peacocks'
eḍj-u	'bear'
eḍjku	'bears'

3.9. -m. Nouns ending in -m are largely loan words from Telugu or "Teluguized" forms of Koya lineage names. Native Koya words ending in -m have alternate forms minus the -m.

Examples: maḍakam ~ maḍaka
pūsam ~ pūse

The change from -a- to -e- in the vowel is common and is probably related in some way to the allophone [ä] before -m. Plurals for lineage names are formed derivatively with the third plural masculine personal pronoun (ōru). The remaining plurals are /-n/, /-ku/, /-k/.

Examples:		
	maḍaka-m	'lineage name'
	maḍakamōru	'Maḍakam people'
	pūsa-m	'lineage name'
	pūsamōru	'Pūsam people'
	tella-m	'lineage name'
	tellamōru	'Tellam people'
	pūne-m	'lineage name'
	pūnemōru	'Pūnem people'
	nijja-m	'truth'
	nijjān ~ nijjāku	'truths'
	paṇḍu-m	'festival'
	paṇḍuk	'festivals'

3.10. -ūru. This suffix is probably related to the third plural masculine personal pronoun (ōru). It occurs with collective or "mass" nouns denoting human aggregates.

Examples:		
	manasuṇḍu	'mankind'
	manasūrku	'men'

It also occurs with numerals from two to seven when these are used to enumerate masculine humans. -ūru also occurs with an alternate form for mother or goddess, tallūru. With the exception of numerals and the latter form, the plural is /-ku/. tallūru has the plural suffix /-ask/. After stems ending in a vowel or -y, ūru has the allomorph vūru.

Examples:		
	āyḍu	'fivc'
	āyvūru	
	mūṇḍu	'three'
	mūvūru	

Before the oblique suffix ūru has the allomorph -ūr.

Examples:	manas-ūru	'mankind'
	manasūrku	'men'
	tall-ūru	'mother, goddess'
	tallask	'mothers'
	band-ūru	'relations'
	bandūrku	'relatives
	ira-vūru	'two'
	venk-ūru	'lineage name'
	ind-ūru	'Hindu'
	indūrku	'Hindus'

3.11. -āl. This suffix denotes mature or high status males. It occurs with all kin terms for males older than ego, names of high status occupations, and may be suffixed to personal names of all males older or of higher status than ego. It also occurs with all lineage names ending in -a, or -o. Nouns in -āl occur only with the plural suffix /-ōru/.

Examples:	annāl	'elder brother'
	annalōru	'elder brothers'
	svāmāl	'swāmi'
	svāmalōru	'swāmis'
	rāmāl	'personal name'
	maṭṭāl	'lineage name'
	maṭṭalōru	'maṭṭas'
	tāmo	'lineage name'
	tāmalōru	'tāmas'

3.12. -āḍi. This suffix occurs with kin terms denoting younger female relatives, the word for cat, names of some birds, and with nouns denoting females. The first set occurs exclusively with the plural /-ask/, the second set occurs with the plural suffixes /-ku/ or /-n/, and the third with the plural suffix /-hku/. -āḍi is probably derived from the noun āṇḍa 'female', for example, āṇḍa pilla, 'female child'.

Examples:	ēnd-āḍi	'younger female cross-cousin'
	ēndask	'younger female cross-cousins'
	ēl-āḍi	'younger sister'
	ēlask	'younger sisters'
	mayy-āḍi	'daughter'
	mayyask	'daughters'
	verk-āḍi	'cat'
	verkāku	'cats'

kāk-āḍi	'crow'
kākāku ~ kākān	'crows'
keriyāḍi	'parrot'
keriyāku ~ keriyān	'parrots'
lēd-āḍi	'young female'
lēvāhku	'young females'
mukk-āḍi	'old woman'
mukkāhku	'old women'

3.13. -uṇḍu is probably derived from the third person masculine singular pronoun (ōṇḍu). It occurs with kin terms denoting males younger than ego, with "particularized' mass nouns denoting human aggregates, with the nouns denoting "spirit" and masculine "deity", with personal names for males younger than ego, and with numerals two, three, and five when these are used to enumerate all categories except nouns denoting mature males. -uṇḍu has allomorphs -ṇḍu, -ḍu, and -uḍu. -uṇḍu occurs after stems ending in a consonant and -ṇḍu after stems ending in a vowel. -ḍu occurs only after the numeral stem for five āy-, āyḍu and as a free variant of -ṇḍu in personal names.

Examples: rāmuḍu ~ rāmuṇḍu
dēvuḍu ~ dēvuṇḍu

Kin terms, "spirit", "deity", occur with the plural suffix /-ask/.

Examples:	tamm-uṇḍu	'younger brother'
	tammask	'younger brothers'
	err-uṇḍu (erv-uṇḍu)	'younger male cross-cousin
	errask	'younger male cross-cousins'
	jīv-uḍu (jīv-uṇḍu)	'spirit'
	jīvask	'spirits'
	dēv-uḍu (dēv-uṇḍu)	'deity'
	dēvask	'deities'
	manas-uṇḍu	'(a) man'
	manasūrku	'men'
	lacc-uḍu (lacc-uṇḍu)	'personal name'
	āy-ḍu	'five'
	mū-ṇḍu	'three'
	re-ṇḍu	'two'

3.14. -ayya. This and the two following forms also function as independent noun stems. As such ayya denotes 'father'. It is suffixed to personal names of males older than ego in free variation with -āl, for example: rāmāl ~ rāmay.

Examples:	rām-ayya	'personal name'
	būc-ayya	'personal name'
	lac(m)-ayya	'personal name'

3.15. -amma. As an independent noun stem this form denotes 'mother's mother'. As a suffix with personal names it denotes females older than ego. Both -ayya and -amma as suffixes are borrowings from Telugu.

Examples:	rām-amma	'personal name'
	būc-amma	'personal name'
	lacc-amma	'personal name'

3.16. -akka denotes 'elder sister' as an independent noun stem. Suffixed to personal names it denotes a female of an age near that of one's elder sister.

Examples:	rām-akka	'personal name'
	lac(m)-akka	'personal name'

3.17. -āri. This form occurs with nouns denoting occupational specialists and in two cases with nouns denoting inanimate objects. The plural is /-hku/ or /-n/.

Examples:	gal-āri	'watchman'
	galāhku	'watchmen'
	pūj-āri	'priest'
	pūjārīn	'priests'
	pūng-āri	'flower'
	pūngāhku	'flowers'
	ēp-āri	'marriage arranger'
	ēpārīn	'marriage arrangers'

3.18. -āli occurs with nouns denoting nonhuman animate objects and inanimate objects. The plural is /-ku/ or /-n/. -āli varies freely with -āl.

Examples:	musekt-āli (musekt-āl)	'mouse'
	musektālīn (musektālku)	'mice'
	gubb-āli (gubb-āl)	'hillock'
	gubbālīn (gubbālku)	'hillocks'

3.19. -uru occurs with two nouns denoting body parts, and three nouns denoting plants or plant parts. The plural suffix is /-ku/.

Examples:	nud-uru	'forehead'
	nudurku	'foreheads'
	nett-uru	'blood'
	vedd-uru	'bamboo'
	veddurku	'bamboos'

3.20. -ava. This set denotes human, nonhuman, animate, and inanimate objects. It occurs with the plural suffix /-ku/ or /-n/.

Examples:	paḍ-ava	'boat'
	paḍavāku	'boats'
	dēn-ava	'mythological cow'

3.21. -ḍa. This is a doubtful morph. There are only two examples, and the preceding vowel which should be part of the suffix is different in each case. The plural is /-ku/.

Examples:	jalle-ḍa	'sieve'
	jalleḍāku	'sieves'
	tema-ḍa	'phleghm'

3.22. -ḍi. This form should also be cited as Vḍi. The preceding vowel is usually o or e, ē. There are only two cases where the vowel is -i and one where it is -a. It occurs with nouns denoting phratries and lineages, girl, bard, various animate and inanimate objects. With the exception of nouns for lineages and phratries, the plural is /-n/ or /-ōru/.

Examples:	pārē-ḍi	'phratry name'
	pīso-ḍi	'lineage name'
	pīki-ḍi	'girl'
	puppo-ḍi	'pollen'
	vēso-ḍi	'tale'
	vēsoḍīn	'tales'
	kāvo-ḍi	'carrying stick'
	kāvoḍīn	'carrying sticks'

3.23. -ta. This form occurs with nouns denoting nonhuman animates, and inanimate objects. The plural suffix is /-ku/ or /-n/.

Examples:	gon-ta	'throat'
	gontāku	'throats'
	miḍu-ta	'locust'
	miḍutāku	'locusts'
	paṇ-ta	'harvest'
	paṇtāku	'harvests'

3.24. -ti. Like the preceding form, this suffix should probably be segmented as Vti. The vowel is either -a or -i. Nouns in this set denote inanimate objects and in one case a lineage. The plural suffix is /-n/ or /-īru/.

Examples:	ara-ti	'banana'
	aratīn	'bananas'
	kaṇi-ti	'wen'
	kaṇitīn	'wens'
	kani-ti	'lineage name'
	kanitīru	'kanis'

3.25. -ke. There are only two instances of this form. In one case it is preceded by a long vowel which may be part of the suffix. The plural suffix is /-n/.

Examples:	nāl-ke	'tongue'
	nālkēn	'tongues'
	kāṭa-ke	'eye make-up'
	kāṭakēn	'eye make-ups'

3.26. -ka. Again the form of this suffix should probably be -Vka. In all but one case, the vowel is -a. In several cases, the suffix occurs with a derivative final -m. Nouns of this set denote both nonhuman animates and inanimate objects, collectives, and qualities. The plural suffix is /-ku/ ~ /-n/.

Examples:	kā-ka	'heat of the sun'
	lona-ka	'dent'
	lonakāku	'dents'
	nār-ka	'night'
	nārkāku	'nights'
	karra-ka	'lineage name'
	karrakalōru	'karras'
	teli-ka	'light' (in weight)
	maḍa-kam	'lineage name'
	maḍakamōru (maḍakamīru)	'maḍas'

3.27. -iki. Members of this set denote both nonhuman animates and inanimate objects. The plural suffix is /-n/.

Examples:	rēy-iki	'woman's jacket'
	rēyikīn	'jackets'
	ēn-iki	'elephant'
	ēnikīn	'elephants'
	kiṭ-iki	'window'
	kiṭikīn	'windows'

3.28. -ku. There are only two instances of this form. Neither occurs with a plural.

Examples:	allu-ku	'cow dung'
	cikā-ku	'doubt'

3.29. -āyi. This form is in free variation in the singular with -āy. Included in this set is one case in which the initial vowel has either been elided or is represented as -i. The nouns denote nonhuman animates and inanimate objects. The plural is /-n/.

Examples:	puḍ-iyi	'worm'
	puḍiyīn	'worms'
	pōg-āyi	'tobacco'
	tupp-āyi	'gun'
	tuppāyīn	'guns'

3.30. -iya. This set includes three forms in which a final -m (iyam) occurs as part of the suffix in free variation with -iya. All cases denote lineage names. The plural suffix is /-īru/.

Examples:	miḍ-iyam	'lineage name'
	miḍiyamīru	'Miḍiyam people'
	moḍ-iyam	'lineage name'
	moḍiyamīru	'Moḍiyam people'
	ār-iyam (sār-iyam)	'lineage name'
	āriyamīru	'Āriyam people'

3.31. -ili. Included in this set are nouns denoting body parts and other inanimate objects. The plural is /-n/.

Examples:	majj-ili	'buttermilk'
	vāk-ili	'door'
	vākilīn	'doors'
	pes-ili	'green'
	ang-ili	'palate'
	angilīn	'palates'

3.32. -ōli. There are only two instances of this form. Both denote animals. The plural is /-n/ or /-ku/.

Examples:	mos-ōli	'crocodile'
	mosōlīn (mosōlku)	'crocodiles'
	mol-ōli	'hare'
	molōlīn	'hares'

3.33. -ūli. Nouns which take this suffix denote animals, body parts, and other inanimate objects. The plural suffix is /-n/ or /-ku/. In the nominative singular this form is in free variation with -ul.

Examples:	ucc-ūli	'spit'
	ucculīn	'spit (pl.)'
	katt-ūli	'cot'
	kattulīn	'cots'
	mēnd-ūli	'back'
	mēndulīn (mēndulku)	'backs'

3.34. -ēli. This set includes nouns denoting animals and inanimate objects. The plural suffix is /-n/ or /-ku/. Like all other forms in Vli and Vyi it is in free variation in the nominative singular with -Vl.

Examples:	tāb-ēli	'tortoise'
	tābēlīn	'tortoises'
	ōd-ēli	'hearth
	ōdēlīn	'hearths'
	dagg-ēli	'kind of plant'
	daggēlīn	'kind of plant (pl.)'
	goḍḍ-ēli	'axe'
	goḍḍēlīn	'axes'

3.35. -īri. Nouns in this set denote only inanimate objects. There is free variation in the nominative singular with -īr. The plural suffix is /-n/.

Examples:	kuss-īri	'curry'
	kussīrīn	'curries'
	epp-īri	'leaf packet'
	eppīrīn	'leaf packets'

3.36. -ēri. Nouns in this set denote only inanimate objects. There is free variation in the nominative singular with -ēr. The plural suffix is /-n/.

Examples:	kinn-ēri	'violin'
	kinnērīn	'violins'
	kass-ēri	'sword, knife'
	kassērīn	'swords, knives'

3.37. -ōri. There are only two instances of this form. One denotes a body part, the other salt. There is free variation in the nominative singular with -or. The plural suffix is /-n/.

moss-ōri	'nostril'
mossorīn	'nostrils'
ovv-ōri	'salt'

3.38. Suffixes are of four classes: (1) plural; (2) oblique; (3) case; (4) postpositions. A noun may occur with all or none of these suffixes. When two or more occur, the order is as given. Noun constructions may thus be formulated as follows:

$$\text{Base} \pm \left\{ \begin{array}{l} \text{oblique} \pm \left\{ \begin{array}{l} \text{case suffixes} \\ \text{postpositions} \pm \text{oblique} \pm \left\{ \begin{array}{l} \text{case suffixes} \\ \text{postpositions} \end{array} \right. \end{array} \right. \\ \\ \text{plural} \pm \text{oblique} \pm \left\{ \begin{array}{l} \text{case suffixes} \\ \text{postpositions} \pm \text{oblique} \end{array} \right. \end{array} \right.$$

3.39. Theoretically, the expansion oblique + postposition + oblique is limited only by semantic appropriateness. In fact, no more than two expansions occur in the corpus.

/lōtaggeṭiki/	'to near the house'
(lōnu + t + agge + ṭ + iki)	

I.e., base + oblique + postposition + oblique + case suffix.

3.40. The plural //-K//; //-oru//. On semantic grounds, there are two plurals: //-K// and //-oru//. //-oru// occurs with all nouns carrying the derivative suffix -āl and with lineage names. It has the following allomorphs: /-ōru/, /-ōlu/, /-ri/, /-īru/, /-ēru/, /-īri/. /-ōlu/ is an infrequent free variant of /-ōru/. /-ōru/ occurs with all nouns ending in the derivative suffix -āl. /-īru/ occurs with all lineage names ending in -m. /-ri/ occurs only with tappe, the intimate term for father. /-ēru/, /-īri/ vary freely with /-īru/, though in one case /-ēru/ occurs after -āl: kōngalēru, 'the Konga people'.

Examples:

Singular		Plural
tātāl	'mother's father'	tātalōru
pūnem	'lineage name'	pūnemīri
tappe	'father'	tappēri
pūsam	'lineage name'	pūsemīru

//-K// is the plural suffix for all other nouns. It has allomorphs: /-k/, /-n/, /-ask/, /-hku/, /-ngu/, /-ku/. /-k/ occurs after all nouns ending in -ngu, -mbu, -rgu, -pu, -V̄ḍu. /-n/ usually occurs after all nouns ending in a front vowel, but there tends to be some variation with /-ku/ especially when other suffixes follow the plural. /-n/ and /-ku/ vary freely after nouns ending in -a. Where derivative suffixes in -Vli have alternate forms in -Vl, /-n/ occurs after -Vli and /-ku/ after /-Vl/ variants. /-n/ also occurs after all nouns ending in -ṇḍi, -ṇḍe, -ṇḍa. /-ask/ occurs after all nouns having the derivative suffix -uṇḍu or one of its allomorphs, after all nouns denoting kinsmen and ending in the derivative suffix -āḍi. It also occurs with nela, the word for 'moon' or 'month'. /-hku/ occurs after all other nouns ending in -āḍi and the following list class: pūngāri 'flower', galāri 'watchman', gorōḍi 'vulture', lōnu 'house', nāru 'village', vēru 'root', rēnu 'footstalk', bāku 'debt', ēru 'water', and Telugu loan words with the suffix -gāru. /-ngu/ occurs only with pani 'work' and nouns ending in -rru, though it occasionally varies with /-ku/ after nouns ending in -a. /-ku/ occurs elsewhere.

Examples:

	Singular		Plural
/-k/	vāngu	'river'	vānguk
	erpu	'sandal'	erpuk
	cembu	'small pot'	cembuk
	tāḍu	'rope'	tāḍuk

	Singular		Plural
/-n/	vīsi	'fly'	vīsīn (vīsīku)
	īte	'spear'	ītēn (ītēku)
	piṭṭe	'bird'	piṭṭēn
	meṭṭa	'mountain'	meṭṭān (meṭṭāku)
	akka	'elder sister'	akkān (akkāku)
	kuṇḍa	'pot'	kunnān
	paṇḍi	'fruit'	paṇṇīn
	gubbāl (gubbāli)	'hillock'	gubbālku (gubbālīn)
	kattul (kattūli)	'cot'	kattulku (kattulīn)
/-ask/	tammuṇḍu	'younger brother'	tammask
	eruṇḍu (erruṇḍu) (ervuṇḍu)	'younger male cross-cousin'	errask
	ēlāḍi	'younger sister'	ēlask
	mayyāḍi	'daughter'	mayyask
	nela	'month, moon'	nelask
/-hku/	nāṭvāḍi	'young woman'	nāṭvāhku
	pūngāri	'flower'	pūngāhku
	lōnu	'house'	lōhku
	rēṇu	'footstalk'	rēhku
	kōḍagāru	'enemy'	kōḍagāhku
/-ngu/	pani	'work'	panungu
	girru	'feather'	girrungu
	māṭa	'word'	(māṭāngu) māṭan, māṭāku
/-ku/	mabbu	'cloud'	mabku
	cēnu	'field'	cēnku
	eḍju	'bear'	eḍjku

3.41. The oblique //-IN//, //-T//. There are two oblique suffixes, //-IN// and //-T//. //-IN// occurs after all nouns ending in -u except those ending in -ssu, -rru, -llu, -vvu and the majority of those of the form (C)VCu. It also occurs after all nouns denoting males. Finally, it occurs before the genitive suffix with all nouns denoting humans and after the plural suffix of all nouns. //-T// occurs after all other nouns.

//-IN// has the following allomorphs: /-n/, /-ϕ/, /-in/. /-n/ occurs after stem allomorphs ending in vowels; /-ϕ/ after the plural suffix /-n/, and /-in/ occurs elsewhere.

Examples:

/-n/	pōyi + //-IN//	pōyīn-	'headman'
	pēka + //-IN//	pēkān-	'boy'
/-in/	koḍuku + //-IN//	koḍukin-	'son'
	eḍju + //-IN//	eḍjin-	'bear'
/-ϕ/	āki + //-K// + //-IN//	ākīn-	'leaves'
	meṭṭa + //-K// + //-IN//	meṭṭān-	'mountains'

The oblique suffix //-T// has allomorphs: /-ṭ/, /-d/, and /-t/. /-ṭ/ occurs after stem allomorphs ending in retroflex consonants, after stems ending in -āri and V̄ḍi, and with nūru 'one-hundred', nāru 'village', vēru 'root', bāku 'debt', ēru 'water'. /-d/ occurs after stems ending in -y, -Vḍi, -rri, -rru, -llu, and V̄Cu. /-t/ occurs elsewhere.

Examples:

/-ṭ/	ēlāḍi + //-T//	ēlāṭ-	'younger sister'
	pūngāri + //-T//	pūngāṭ-	'flower'
	vēru + //-T//	vēṭ-	'root'
/-d/	nāy + //-T//	nāyd-	'dog'
	girru + //-T//	gird-	'feather'
	baḍi + //-T//	baḍid-	'school'
	pāmu + //-T//	pāmd-	'snake'
	arri + //-T//	ard-	'path'
/-t/	meṭṭa + //-T//	meṭṭāt-	'mountain'
	kīke + //-T//	kīkēt-	'fish'

Some nouns occur in the singular with either //-T// or //-IN//. Other than the restriction that //-T// never occurs with nouns denoting males, there is no formal criterion for making a precise statement. Most of the variation, however, seems to be for //-IN// to occur before the genitive suffix and //-T// before other case suffixes and postpositions. This may indicate that //-IN// should more appropriately be segmented as a simple genitive and not as an oblique suffix. This is strengthened by the fact that nouns ending in -āḍi and denoting human females form an oblique stem with //-T// before an allomorph of the genitive (-ini). This allomorph looks suspiciously like the oblique //-IN// and the genitive suffix /-i/. Yet, since it is easier to say that case suffixes occur after an oblique stem than to say that they occur after the oblique or genitive stems, I prefer to regard //-IN// as an oblique suffix rather than part of the genitive. Alternatively, one could segment the genitive suffix /-a/ which always occurs after //-T// as /-ta/. This makes some sense especially since //-T// before postpositions beginning with consonants sometimes seems to have a vowel -a between the oblique and the postposition.

Example: meṭṭāt(a)porrot(a)nunci 'from on the mountain'

Obviously, I leave the problem unresolved. For a discussion of similar problems with the oblique and genitive, see: 3.49 and Emeneau (1955:31, 61).

3.42. Case suffixes. Case suffixes include a genitive, a dative, an accusative, an instrumental locative, an ablative, and a sociative instrumental. The nominative is equivalent to the uninflected stem. For the use of cases, see 5.3.

3.43. The genitive suffix //I//. The genitive denotes possession of whatever the preceding noun denotes. It has three allomorphs: /-i/, /-ini/, and /-a/. Except as noted below, the latter occurs after stems forming the oblique with //-T //. /-ini/ occurs after nouns denoting females or ending in -āḍi (cf. 3.41). /-i/ occurs after stems forming the oblique with //IN//.

Examples:

/-i/	//tappe + IN + I//	/tappēni/	'father's'
/-ini/	//mayyāḍi + T + I//	/mayyāṭini/	'daughter's'
/-a/	//mallu + T + I//	/malda/	'peacock's'

3.44. The dative suffix //IKI//. The dative indicates 'to' or 'for' the preceding noun. It has the following allomorphs: /-ku/, /-iki/, /-ki/. /-ku/ occurs after the oblique forms of the first and second person singular and plural pronouns. /-iki/ occurs after the oblique allomorphs /-ṭ/, /-d/, and in the singular after the oblique allomorph /-n/. /-ki/ occurs elsewhere.

Examples:

/-ku/	/nāku/	'to me'
	/mīku/	'to you'
/-iki/	/pūngāṭiki/	'to the flower'
	/nāydiki/	'to the dog'
	/tappēniki/	'to the father'
/-ki/	/kāykinki/	'to hands'
	/meṭṭātki/	'to mountains'

3.45. The accusative suffix //NI//. The accusative denotes the direct object of the verb. Its allomorphs are: /-nni/, /-minni/, /-ninni/, /-ini/, /-i/. /-nni/ occurs after the third person masculine singular and plural pronouns. /-minni/ occurs after the first person plural inclusive pronoun. /-ninni/ occurs after the first and second person singular pronouns. /-i/ occurs after all oblique forms in //-IN//. /-ini/ occurs elsewhere. Only on syntactic grounds is the accusative allomorph /-i/ distinguishable from the genitive.

Examples:	pantulini pelli arte	'she married a school master' (accusative)
	pantulini ēlask	'school master's younger sisters' (genitive)

/-nni/	//ōnḍu + IN + NI//	/ōninni/	'him'
/-minni/	//mannaḍa + IN + NI//	/māminni/	'us'
/-ninni/	//nimma + IN + NI//	/nīninni/	'you'
/-i/	//tappe + IN + NI//	/tappēni/	'father'
	//eḍju + IN + NI//	/eḍjini/	'bear'
/-ini/	//meṭṭa + T + NI//	/meṭṭātini/	'mountain'

3.46. The instrumental locative suffix //E//. //E// has no allomorphs. It denotes either the location 'in', 'inside', or the instrumentality 'by', 'by means of', 'with'.

Examples:	goḍḍēlīte	'with an ax'
	lōte	'in the house'
	banḍīte	'with, in an oxcart'
	eḍjine	'in a bear'
	nāhkine	'in villages'
	kāykine	'in hands'
	avvite	'in them'

//E// does not occur with kin terms, nouns denoting humans, nor personal pronouns with the exception of the third person neuter singular and plural. Instrumentality in these cases is expressed by kāyde ('with hand') following the genitive suffix.

Example: ōni kāyde 'by him'

Location is expressed by various postpositions.

Example: ōni lōpala 'inside him'

Other locative concepts occurring with all nouns are also expressed by postpositions.

3.47. The ablative suffix //-KASI//. The ablative denotes 'place from'. It has three free variants: /-kāsi/, /-kunci/, /-nunci/. The last two are borrowings from Telugu. Segmentation is a problem here since /-kāsi/ and /-kunci/ are derivable from dative /-ki/ plus the past passive participle of ā- 'to become' and unc- 'to keep'. Thus literally 'having become, having remained to there'. /-nunci/ is probably the oblique /-n/ plus the past participle of unc- 'to keep'. Historically and comparatively, this segmentation is correct, yet it creates problems descriptively. The standard oblique for gubbāl 'hillock', e.g., is //T//. Thus, gubbāltkāsi 'from hillock', but also gubbāltnunci 'from hillock'. One would expect gubbālnunci. For reasons of this sort, the ablative forms are given here in unsegmented form.

Examples:	bajjārtkāsi	'from the bazaar'
	aḍivitkunci	'from the forest'
	bastārtnunci	'from Bastar'
	gubbāltnunci	'from the hillock'

With the names of towns and regions, the ablative sometimes occurs directly following the nominative form of the noun rather than the oblique.

Example: hāyderabādnunci 'from Hyderabad'

The ablative is the only case suffix which may be suffixed to another case suffix—the locative.

Example: lōtenunci 'from in the house'

These peculiarities are all the result of derivation from a verb form which would normally occur in phrase final position. Yet since none of the ablative forms occurs independently either as verbs or nouns, the only alternative would be to treat them as adverbial forms. This would not be a better solution since adverbial suffixes do not follow oblique stems.

3.48. The sociative instrumental suffix //-TONTE//. This suffix denotes 'along with', 'with', 'by', 'by means of'. It occurs less frequently as an instrumental. //-TONTE// has two allomorphs: /-tōṇṭe/ and /-ōṇṭe/. The latter occurs with personal pronouns and nouns forming the oblique in //IN//. /-tōṇṭe/ occurs elsewhere. Again segmentation is a problem, for /-tōṇṭe/ is probably a compound form comprised of the oblique //T// + /ōṇṭe/. The final

/-e/ may be the instrumental suffix. If the form be analyzed simply as /tōṇṭe/ without allomorphs, then interpretation would be difficult. In some cases /-tōṇṭe/ would occur suffixed to the oblique stem and in others suffixed directly to the nominative stem or an allomorph of the oblique. Since this is complex, I have chosen to analyze the suffix as being represented by two allomorphs.

Examples:	nātoṇṭe	'along with me'
	dānitōṇṭe	'along with her, it'
	goddeltōṇṭe	'with an axe'
	kasseṭoṇṭe	'with a knife'

3.49. Postpositions (Po). On formal grounds, postpositions are differentiated from case suffixes because they may be inflected with case suffixes and because they may occur as independent noun forms. Thus, case suffixes are bound and cannot be expanded by other case suffixes or postpositions (for exceptions, see 3.48). Postpositions differ from other nouns by the fact that they can be suffixed to the oblique forms of other noun stems.

The most frequently occurring postpositions are:

porro	'on, over, above'
perke	'after'
sēnka	'for sake of'
kosam	'for sake of'
valla	'by means of'
kāyde (kāy + T + E)	'by means of, with' (3.46)
lōpala ~ lōpa	'inside, within'
payya	'after, afterwards, later'
agga	'near'
pakka	'beside, near, next to'
venuka	'behind'
iḍupo	'under, down, below, beneath'
pāy	'above, over'
dānka	'up to, until, at the time of'
vēlu	'time, time of'

Examples:	paṇṇīn sēnka	'for sake of fruit'
	meṭṭātporro	'on (the) mountain'
	lōtagga	'near house'
	martiḍupo	'under (the) tree'

It is difficult to determine whether postpositions are suffixed to the oblique or adjective form of a noun. In slow speech a vowel frequently intervened between the oblique and the initial consonant of a postposition, but disappeared in rapid speech. This is but one more aspect of the general difficulty of segmenting adjectives, postpositions and genitives. For analytic convenience, I have assumed that postpositions are added to the oblique base.

3.50. Number and gender subclasses. Nouns are differentiated from other form classes by the occurrence of more than one form to which the same set of suffixes may be added. Nouns may be divided into subclasses on the basis of the number and types of forms to which case suffixes may be added. There are six classes consisting of items with: (1) one singular, one plural; (2) two singulars, one plural; (3) two singulars, two plurals; (4) two plurals, no singular; (5) two or more singulars, no plural; (6) personal pronouns. Class four includes only the numerals from two on and the numerals for 'this many', 'that many', 'how many'. Class five includes the numeral one. Class one includes the majority of nouns. Class two includes the interrogative and indefinite pronouns and some nouns with derivative suffixes -uṇḍu, -ūru. Class three includes all nouns denoting humans with derivative suffixes -āḍi-, -ōṇḍu, -ōru, -āl, and nouns derived from adjectives.

3.51. Except for nouns denoting male humans, all class one nouns are feminine neuter. Examples of class one have been given in 3.40.

3.52. Class two nouns have either two masculine and feminine forms in the singular and one form undifferentiated for gender in the plural or one masculine/feminine and one masculine form in the singular with one undifferentiated form in the plural.

Examples:	Singular		Plural
f.	bēdu/bēnō	'who'	
m.	bēnōṇḍu/bēnō	'who'	bēnōru
m.	manasuṇḍu	'a man'	
m.f.	manasūru	'mankind'	manasūrku
f.	bandu	'relative'	
m.	banduṇḍu	'relative'	
m.f.	bandūru	'relation'	bandūrku

The form manisi which sometimes alternates with manasuṇḍu or manasūru could be taken as a differentiated female form, but it is only a borrowing from Telugu which overlaps the masculine/feminine distinction. Occasionally, a separate feminine plural was used for bandu: bandurāl(u). This again, is a borrowing from Telugu.

3.53. Class three contains nouns denoting humans, including personal names, and nouns derived from adjectives. Class three nouns distinguish masculine and feminine in both singular and plural, or masculine singular/plural from feminine/neuter singular/plural.

Examples:	Singular		Plural
m.	lēyōṇḍu	'young man'	lēyōru
f.	lēdāḍi	'young woman'	lēvāhku
m.	mukkāl	'old man'	mukkalōru
f.	mukkāḍi	'old woman'	mukkāhku
m.	muccatōṇḍu	'leper'	muccatōru
f/n.	muccaṭi	'leper'	muccāku
m.	vādanōṇḍu	'man who came'	vādanōru
f/n.	vādanaddu	'one who came'	vādanavvu
m.	buccuḍu	'personal name'	buccāl (buccayya)

	Singular		Plural
f.	bucci	'personal name'	buccamma
m.	rāmuḍu	'personal name'	rāmāl (rāmmaya)
f.	rāmi	'personal name'	rāmamma

On syntactic grounds, inclusion of personal names in this category is a bit strained. One may, for example, address and refer to a male familiarly as bucci, yet in a sentence referring to a male bucci, the verb ending is either masculine singular or masculine plural, usually the former.

Example: bucci vāyitōṇḍu 'bucci (male) will come'

This contrasts with

bucci vāyīte 'bucci (female) will come'

On the other hand, the feminine/neuter plural does not occur with the verb when -amma is used.

Example: buccamma vāyīte 'buccamma will come'

This contrasts with

buccāl vāyitōru 'buccāl will come'

vāyitōru has the masculine plural personal ending -ōru. All of this is consistent with the masculine aspect of class three, but is inconsistent in the female component. On the analogy of lēydādi vāyīte 'the young woman will come', and lēvāku vāyitāku 'the young women will come', one would expect agreement between noun plural and plural verb personal ending. But, contrast bucci vāyīte, buccamma vāyīte. A part of the problem here is that -ayya and -amma are recent borrowings from Telugu. This tends to partially skew the Koya masculine singular/plural versus feminine/neuter singular/plural distribution in the direction of the Telugu masculine singular versus feminine/neuter singular and masculine/feminine plural versus neuter plural system. A similar shift is apparent in the numeral forms used in enumerating masculine persons (-vūru and -mandi 3.54, see 3.52). Another aspect of the problem is that my assumption of an identity between plurality and respect/formality may be incorrect. For a further discussion of this point, see Tyler, 1965.

3.54. Class four nouns have no singular and are differentiated by separate plural forms for feminine/neuter and masculine. Up to the number eight, the plural form for masculine nouns is -vūru. From eight on and for 'this many', 'that many', 'how many', -mandi is suffixed to the numeral stem to denote masculine persons.

Examples:	f/n.	reṇḍu nāṭvāhku	'two young women'
	f/n.	reṇḍu eṭku	'two trees'
	m.	iruvūru tātalōru	'two mother's fathers'
	f/n.	ennimidi nāṭvāhku	'eight young women'
	f/n.	ennimidi eṭku	'eight trees'
	m.	ennimidi mandi tātalōru	'eight mother's fathers'

Only numerals ending in -(ṇ)ḍu have allomorphs before the suffix -vūru. These are given below:

reṇḍu / + vūru // ira-

{ muṇḍu / āyḍu } / + vūru // { mū- / āy- }

The numerals denoting 'this many', 'that many', 'how many' are similarly differentiated on the basis of feminine/neuter versus masculine.

Examples:	feminine/neuter		masculine
	icco	'this many'	icco mandi
	becco	'how many'	becco mandi
	acco	'that many'	acco mandi

In addition to the form acco, anta (a borrowing from Telugu) occurs. In this case, the masculine suffix is -ōru.

Example:	anta	'that many'	andōru

There tends to be variation in all the numerals between a differentiation of feminine/neuter versus masculine and a differentiation of neuter versus masculine/feminine. I think the latter type derives from Telugu usage. The remaining numerals are listed as follows:

orro	'one'	padihēḍu	'seventeen'
reṇḍu	'two'	padennimidi	'eighteen'
mūṇḍu	'three	padtommidi	'nineteen'
nālu	'four	iravāy	'twenty'
āyḍu	'five'	iravāyorro	'twenty-one'
āru	'six'	muppāy	'thirty'
ēḍu	'seven'	nalabāy	'forty'
ennimidi	'eight'	yābāy	'fifty'
tommidi	'nine'	āruvāy	'sixty'
padi	'ten	debbāy	'seventy'
padakonda	'eleven'	ennabāy	'eighty'
panendu	'twelve'	tombāy	'ninety'
padimūṇḍu	'thirteen'	nūru	'one hundred'
padnālugu	'fourteen'	nūtorro	'one hundred one'
padihēnu	'fifteen'	nūtimūṇḍu	'one hundred three'
padahāru	'sixteen'	vanda	'one hundred'

With the exception of one, three, and four, these are identical with Telugu numerals. It is apparent that tens are based on the numeral ten plus one of the other numerals from one to ten, but the allomorphy is so complex here that no attempt at more refined analysis is made. Ten, for example, has the allomorphs padi, pata, pan, pad. Similar difficulties occur with stem allomorphs before the suffix -vāy which itself has allomorphs -ppāy, -bāy, -bbāy, -pāy. The numeral four has an allomorph nāga ~ nānga in the compound nāgavēlu 'fourth day of the marriage ceremony.'

Ordinals are formed by suffixing -ō to the stem, with the exception of the numeral one, which has the form modati ('first').

Examples:	reṇḍō	'second'
	muṇḍō	'third'
	nālō	'fourth'
	āydō	'fifth'

All numerals from one to seven and those for 'this many', 'how many', 'just this way', 'just that way', 'just what way', etc. can be expanded by the suffix -ṭi added to the ordinal form. For one, -ṭi is added to the cardinal stem. This should probably be interpreted as a "nominalizing" neuter personal ending suffix. The general meaning varies between that of an ordinal and denoting just whatever the numeral indicates.

Examples:	orrōṭi	'first', 'just one'
	reṇḍōṭi	'second', 'just two'
	beccōṭi	'just how many'
	iccōṭi	'just this many'
	accōṭi	'just that many'
	antaṭi	'just that many'

Except for those denoting one hundred, numerals form their oblique on the ordinal. The oblique suffix for all but vanda ('one hundred') is /-t/; vanda has /-n/.

Examples: āyḍu vandāni kōya lēyōṇḍu 'five hundred kōya youths'
nūṭorro (nūru + t + orro) rūpāyīn 'one hundred one rupees'

The distribution for vanda and nūru is not certain, but seems to be nūru from one hundred to one hundred ninety-nine, and vanda from two hundred on.

3.55. The only noun in class five is the numeral one. It has separate forms for masculine and feminine/neuter.

Example:	f/n. orro	'one'
	m. orrōṇḍu	'one male'

3.56. Class six—pronouns. Pronouns (PN) form a separate class since they can be expanded by a prior attribute of the same class (i.e., with personal pronouns) only in restricted semantic domains; for example: mā ōru 'my husband' (literally, 'our, they'). The pronouns are personal, reflexive, interrogative, and indefinite.

Personal pronouns. The personal pronouns have the following independent and oblique forms:

	Independent	Oblique
1st sing.	nanna	nā
1st pl. (exclusive)	manna	mā
1st pl. (inclusive)	mannaḍa	manna
2nd sing.	nimma	nī
2nd pl.	mīru	mī

	Independent	Oblique
3rd sing. m.	ōṇḍu	ōni
3rd pl. m.	ōru	ōri
3rd. sing.f/n.	addu	dāni
3rd. pl. f/n.	avvu	vāṇi, vāṇṭ-, avvi

All third person pronouns have contrasting proximate forms as follows:

sing. m.	vīṇḍu	vīni
pl. m.	vīru	vīri
sing. f/n.	iddu	dīni
pl. f/n.	ivvu	vīṭi, ivvi

vāru infrequently varies with ōru, especially in its oblique form vāri. Both vāru and mīru are recent borrowings from Telegu. No attempt is made to analyze personal pronouns into stems and suffixes, though it is apparent that all third person pronouns have some form of demonstrative adjective prefixed to the stem.

Reflexive pronouns. Reflexive pronouns occur only infrequently. The independent singular and plural and the oblique plural never occurred in text and were given only under extreme eliciting.

	Independent	Oblique
sing.	tān	tan
pl.	tām	tam

Interrogative pronouns. Interrogatives are derived from personal pronouns preceded by the interrogative demonstrative adjective base, bē or bēn.

	Independent	Oblique
3rd sing. f/n.	bēdu	bēni
3rd sing. m.	bēnōṇḍu	bēnōni
3rd pl. m.	bēnōru	bēnōri

bēnōṇḍu has free variants: bēnō, bōnō.

Indefinite pronouns. With the exception of bēdu, the indefinite is formed by adding the suffix -anna to the independent stem of the interrogative. bēdu forms its indefinite with the dubitative clitic -ō (3.80).

3rd sing. f/n.	bēdō	'whatever', 'something', 'whoever'
3rd sing. m.	bēnōṇḍanna	'whoever', 'somebody'
3rd pl. m.	bēnōranna	'whoever', 'somebody'

3.58. Noun classes based on stem allomorphy. Noun bases have allomorphs before plural and oblique suffixes. Twelve inflectional classes are derived from this allomorphy.

3.59. Class one. Class one consists of noun bases in (C)VCCu (where CC is any geminated consonant except -r). There are two subclasses based on oblique formation. Subclass (a) occurs before the oblique //IN//, subclass (b) before the oblique //T//.

Basic Stem		Stem Alternate before Suffix Class //K//	//T//	//IN//
(a) addu	'order'	ad-		add-
mabbu	'cloud'	mab-		mabb-
goḍḍu	'cow'	goḍ-		goḍḍ-
vinnu	'heaven'	vin-		vinn-
(b) mallu	'peacock'	mal-	mal-	
kevvu	'ear'	kev-	kev-	
appu	'loan'	ap-	ap-	
kissu	'fire'	kis-	kis-	

One -i ending noun also belongs in subclass (b); pelli 'marriage' pel-. One noun, duvvu 'tiger', occurs before both oblique suffixes. It has allomorphs: duv-, dūv-, duvv-.

3.60. Class two: Nouns in this class have the following shapes: (C)VCVCu, (C)V̄CVCu, (C)VCCVCu, (C)VCCu, (C)V̄Cu. Final CC is any consonant cluster other than a geminate, or -ṇḍ, -ng, -np, -mb, -rg. Only nouns in (C)V̄Cu occur before //T//. For exceptions to subclass (b), see 3.62.

Basic Stem		Stem Alternate before Suffix Class //K//	//T//	//IN//
(a) eḍju	'bear'	eḍj-		eḍj-
kandu	'eye'	kand-		kand-
rōju	'day'	rōj-		rōj-
kōḍuku	'son'	kōḍuk-		kōḍuk-
karuvu	'hunger'	karuv-		karuv-
bandūru	'relations'	bandūr		bandūr-
(b) cēnu	'field'	cēn-	cēn-	
tōlu	'skin'	tōl-	tōl-	
kōru	'tusk'	kōr-	kōr-	

3.61. Class three. This class includes all nouns ending in vowels other than -u, with the following restrictions: nouns ending in -ḍi, -ṇḍi, -V̄li, and non-masculine nouns in -ri are excluded. There are three subclasses.

Basic Stem		Stem Alternate before Suffix Class //K//	//T//	//IN//
(a) meṭṭa	'mountain'	meṭṭā-	meṭṭā-	
mēga	'cloud'	mēgā-	mēgā-	
ōḍa	'boat'	ōḍā-	ōḍā-	
bōḍe	'trunk'	bōḍē-	bōḍē-	
āki	'leaf'	ākī-	ākī-	
toḍime	'leaf'	toḍimē-	toḍimē-	
(b) amma	'father's mother'	ammā-	ammā-	ammā-
pilla	'child'	pillā-	pillā-	pillā-
akka	'elder sister'	akkā-	akkā-	akkā-

	Basic Stem		Stem Alternate before Suffix Class //K//	//T//	//IN//
	muṭṭe	'wife'	muṭṭē-	muṭṭē-	muṭṭē-
	kāko	'mother's mother	kākō-	kākō-	kākō-
	pōye	'father's sister'	pōyē-	pōyē-	pōyē-
(c)	tappe	'father'	tappē-		tappē-
	pōyi	'headman'	pōyī-		pōyī-
	pūjāri	'priest'	pūjārī		pūjārī
	marri	'son'	marrī-		marrī-
	āṇe	'sister's son'	āṇē-		āṇē-
(d)	anna	'elder brother'	ann-		annā-
	bāṭo	'elder male cross-cousin	bāṭ-		bāṭō-
	tāto	'mother's father'	tāt-		tātō-
	dādo	'father's father'	dād-		dādō-
	pēka	'male child'	pēk-		pēkā-

Subclasses (b), (c), and (d) are comprised of nouns denoting kin and masculine occupations. All of class (b) are feminine, those of (c) and (d) masculine. marri in subclass (c) has a free variant mar- before the plural suffix.

3.62. Class four includes all monosyllabic nouns in final y.

Basic Stem		Stem Alternate before Suffix Class //K//	//T//	//IN//
nāy	'dog'	nāy-	nāy-	
kāy	'hand'	kāy-	kāy-	

3.63. Class five. This class consists of a small irregular list class in (C)V̄Cu and nouns with the derivative suffix -gāru.

Basic Stem		Stem Alternate before Suffix Class //K//	//T//	//IN//
kōḍagāru	'enemy'	koḍagā-		koḍagā-
lōnu	'house'	lō-	lō-	lō-
nāru	'village'	nā-	nā-	
vēru	'root'	vē-	vē-	
bāku	'debt'	bā-	bā-	
ēru	'water'	ē-	ē-	

I am still uncertain about the oblique stem for this class. In some cases, there seemed to be an [ɦ] before the oblique.

Example: [nāɦṭ-] ~ [nāṭ-].

If the [ɦ] actually occurs, the plural suffix /-hku/ would have to be segmented simply as /-ku/.

3.64. Class six. Included in this class are nouns ending in -ēli, -ōli, -āli, -ūli, -ōri, -ūri, -ēri, -īri.

Basic Stem		Stem Alternate before Suffix Class //K//	//T//
mussōri	'nostril'	mussōrī-	mussōr-
ovvōri	'salt'	ovvōrī-	ovvōr-
peddēri	'name'	peddērī-	peddēr-
molōli	'hare'	molōlī-	molōl-
gubbāli	'hillock'	gubbālī-	gubbāl-
uccūli	'saliva'	uccūlī-	uccūl-
mosōli	'crocodile'	mosōlī-	mosōl-
kastūri	'camphor'	kastūrī-	kastūr-
goḍḍēli	'axe'	goḍḍēlī-	goḍḍēl-
mēndūli	'back'	mēndūlī-	mēndūl-
kussīri	'curry'	kussīrī-	kussīr-

3.65. Class seven includes nouns ending in -V̄ḍi and non-masculine nouns in -āri.

Basic Stem		Stem Alternate before Suffix Class //K//	//T//
keriyāḍi	'parrot'	keriyā-	keriyā-
verkāḍi	'cat'	verkā-	verkā-
gōrōḍi	'vulture'	gōrō-	gōrō-
nāṭvāḍi	'young woman'	nāṭvā-	nāṭvā-
mukkāḍi	'old woman'	mukkā-	mukkā-
pūngāri	'flower'	pūngā-	pūngā-

The following are irregular in this class.

Basic Stem		Stem Alternate before Suffix Class //K//	//T//
ēlāḍi	'younger sister'	ēl-	ēlā-
ēndāḍi	'younger female cross-cousin'	ēnd-	ēndā-
pōdāḍi	'reflexive term used between sisters of the husband and sisters of the wife'	pōd-	pōdā-
mayyāḍi	'daughter'	mayy-	mayyā-
lēdāḍi	'adolescent female'	lēvā-	lēdā-

3.66. Class eight. This class consists of nouns ending in -uṇḍu and -uḍu-

Basic Stem		Stem Alternate before Suffix Class //K//	//IN//
tammuṇḍu	'younger brother'	tamm-	tammu-
erruṇḍu	'younger male cross-cousin'	err-	erru- (eravu-)

Basic Stem		Stem Alternate before Suffix Class //K//	//IN//
manasuṇḍu	'man'	manas-	manasu-
dēvuḍu	'god'	dēv-	dēvu-
jīvuḍu	'soul'	jīv-	jīvu-

Alternatively, with the exception of lēdāḍi, irregular nouns from class seven could be included in this set. Both sets could also be subsumed under subclass (d) of class three.

3.67. Class nine. This class consists of nouns ending in -ṇḍi, -ṇḍe, and -ṇḍa.

Basic Stem		Stem Alternate before Suffix Class //K//	//T//
baṇḍi	'cart'	baṇṇī-	baṇḍī-
paṇḍi	'fruit'	paṇṇī-	paṇḍī-
bottumiṇḍe	'elbow'	bottumiṇṇī-	bottumiṇḍē-
koṇḍa	'ox'	koṇṇā-	koṇḍā-
kuṇḍa	'large clay pot'	kunnā-	kuṇḍā-

3.68. Class ten. This class includes all nouns ending in -m, except those denoting exogamous divisions.

Basic Stem		Stem Alternate before Suffix Class //K//	//T//
vēngālam	'leopard'	vēngālā-	vēngālā-
paṇḍum	'festival'	paṇḍū-	paṇḍū-
nijjam	'truth'	nijjā-	nijjā-
tarram	'generation'	tarrā-	tarrā-

Irregular in this class is pāpam 'sin'. It has the following alternate before both plural and oblique: pāpō-. A broader analysis would include this class as a subclass of class three.

3.69. Class eleven. This class contains nouns ending in -rri- and -rru.

Basic Stem		Stem Alternate before Suffix Class //K//	//T//
arri	'path'	arri-	ar-
girru	'feather'	girru-	gir-

3.70. Class twelve. Included in class twelve are nouns ending in -mbu, -ngu, -rgu, -npu.

Basic Stem		Stem Alternate before Suffix Class //K//	//T//	//IN//
cembu	'metal pot'	cembu-	cembi-	cemb-
vāngu	'river'	vāngu-	vāngi-	vāng-
tēnpu	'fart'	tēnpu-	tēnpi-	tēnp-

3.71. In addition to those previously listed with the appropriate class, four other nouns have irregular formations.

Basic Stem		Stem Alternate before Suffix Class //K//	//T//
būmi	'earth'	būm-	būm-
ḍāmuri	'hawk'	ḍāmō-	ḍāmu-
pani	'work'	panī- (pan-)	pan-
puḍiyi	'worm'	puḍu-	puḍiyi- (puḍu-)

3.72. Noun expansions. (Nn). Nouns and pronouns may be expanded by a prior attribute or by reduplication. The prior attribute may be another noun with or without a possessive suffix, an adjective, or a numeral. Reduplication has two forms: simple repetition and echo words (Ew). Expansion types are given formulaically below.

(1) ST:N + ST:N

Examples:

N	N
rēla 'rēla	pāṭa song'
mōga 'male	pilla child'
ākāsa 'sky	tappe father'
araṭi 'banana	eṭṭu tree'

(2) ST:N + ST:PN

Examples:

N	PN	
pani 'work	vāru they'	'workers'
vaṇṭa 'cook	vāṇḍu he'	'cook'
gaṭṭi 'strong	vāṇḍu he'	'strong man'

(3) ST:N + OBLIQUE + GENITIVE + PN

Examples:

N	OBL	GEN	PN
(dēse	t	a´	ōru)
/dēse	t		ōru/
country			people (they)

N	OBL	GEN	PN	
(segga	t	a´	ōru)	
/segga	t		ōru/	
some			people	'some people'
			(they)	

(4) ST:N + OBLIQUE + GENITIVE + N

Examples:

Pos. PN			N	
/mā			annāl/	'my (our) elder brother'
our			elder brother	

N	OBL	GEN	N	
/muttē	n	i	vijja/	'wife's lineage' (lit. 'wife's seed')
/kis	t	a	gunda/	'hole of fire'
fire			hole	

(5) ST:Adj + $\left\{\begin{array}{l} \text{PN} \\ \text{N} \end{array}\right.$

Examples:

Adj.	N	
/beriya	manasuṇḍu/	'big man'
big	man	
/mukemanna	pustakam/	'important book'
important	book	
/ā	pani/	'that work'
that	work	
Pos. PN	**PN**	
/nā	di/	'mine'
my	it	

(6) ST:V + Adj + $\left\{\begin{array}{l} \text{PN} \\ \text{N} \end{array}\right.$ (cf. 4.6 (9))

Examples:

V	Adj.	N	
/mirt	a	pilla/	'child who ran'
ran		child	
/talap	āni	mukkāl	'old man who asks'
asks		old man	
		PN	
(kett	a´	ōṇḍu)	
/kett		ōṇḍu/	'one who told'
told		he	

(7) ST:Numeral + { PN / N }

Examples:

Num	N	
/ orro	manasuṇḍu/	'one (a) man'
one	man	
/ reṇḍu	mēkān/	'two goats'
two	goats	
	PN	
/ orrō	ṭi/	'one (thing)'
one	it	

(8) Four nouns have specialized meanings in expanded constructions. Structurally they are simply noun compounds similar to (1), (2), (3) above.

ST:N + { anta 'all, whole' / eḍu 'full' }

ST:N + OBLIQUE + GENITIVE + { anta 'all, whole' / kanna 'than' / kante 'than' }

Examples:

N	N	
/ pani	anta/	'all work
work	all	
(kuṇḍa´	anta)	'whole pot'
/ kuṇḍ	anta/	
pot	whole	
(lōhku´	anta)	'all houses'
/ lōhk	anta/	
houses	all	
(gampa´	eḍu)	'basketful'
/ gamp	eḍu/	
basket	full	
(piḍiki´	eḍu)	'fistful, handful'
/ pidik	eḍu/	
fist	full	
(baṇḍi´	eḍu)	'cartful'
/ baṇḍ	eḍu/	
cart	full	
(doppa´	eḍu)	'leafful'
/ dopp	eḍu/	
leaf	full	

N	OBL	GEN	N	
/kassēr knife	t	a	kanna/ than	'than knife'
/kassēr knife	t	a	kante/ than	'than knife'

kanna and kante are used in comparative constructions.

Example: ī kassērtakanna, ā kassēri mancidi 'that knife is better than this knife' (Lit., this knife than, that knife good it.)

Occasionally reṇḍu ('two') and iruvūru ('two males') rather than preceding the modified noun follow it on a pattern analagous to that of antā, eḍu, etc.

Example:

/ēlāḍi	reṇḍu/	'two younger sisters'
younger sister	two, both	'both younger sisters'

Note that this construction does not show agreement in number as would be the case when the numeral precedes the noun.

(9) Reduplication. Simple repetition of nouns is not common, but when it occurs, serves as an intensifier.

Examples:

mēkān mēkān	'goats and goats'
eṭku eṭku	'trees and trees'

Much more frequent is the use of echo words. These are of two types: (1) a noun in the nominative followed by a "meaningless word" similar in phonetic composition to the preceding noun; (2) a sequence of two phonetically similar words which have no meaning independent of the compound construction. Some echo words are simply "poetic" devices, while others add special significance to the preceding noun.

Examples:

Type 1

pillānjillān	'children and children'
kussīri ille gussīri ille	'no curry at all'
kūli nāli	'cooly work'

Type 2

tindo tondo	'every which way'
bōndo bōndo	'stark naked'
incu mincu	'approximately'

The initial constituent of the latter expression is probably somehow derived from uccutu 'a little bit'.

3.73. Qualifiers. Syntactically, qualifiers are attributive words preceding the noun or verb they qualify. Qualifiers agree with the head noun neither in person nor number. Qualifiers in attributive position to a noun are adjectives (Adj.), and those in attributive position to a verb are adverbs (Adv.). Qualifiers are either monomorphemic or complex.

3.74. Monomorphemic adjectives. Monomorphemic adjectives consist of words unanalyzable into constituent morphemes. Included in this class are: demonstrative adjectives, numeral adjectives, and qualitative adjectives.

The demonstrative adjectives are: ī 'this', ā 'that', ē 'which'.

Examples:

ī nāru	'this village'
ā lēyōṇḍu	'that youth'
ē lōnu	'which house'

Numeral adjectives are limited to those denoting 'much':

becku	'how much'
icku	'this much'
acku	'that much'

acku varies freely with anta in attributive constructs. It is apparent that the initial constituents of these are the demonstrative adjectives, but since -cku does not occur in any other construction, the forms are listed here rather than under derivatives. The form uccutu 'a bit' and its reduplicated form uccutucctu 'a tiny bit' belongs here as well. In fact, all words denoting 'much' are probably derived from uccutu (ucc + plural - ku = ucku?).

Qualitative adjectives are quite rare and so far as I can discover limited to the following:

cinna ~ cinni	'small, little'
periya	'large, big'
menci ~ manci	'good'
nalla	'black'
tella	'white'
erra	'red'
pulla	'sour'
tiyya ~ tīya	'sweet'

There are some complications with the color terms and the words for sweet and sour, for all of these may occur with adjectival suffixes (3.75).

The forms cited above would thus appear to be nouns in attributive position similar to expanded noun constructions (3.72). Yet, each also occurs with the nominalizing suffix -ṭi.

Example: ī pālu pullaṭi 'this milk (is) sour'

In constructions of this type -ṭi transforms adjectives into nouns and the above utterance is equivalent to: ī pālu pulla pālu 'this milk (is) sour milk'. This contrasts with: iddu pullana pālu 'this is sour milk'. which varies freely with: iddu pulla pālu 'this is sour milk'.

The situation is further complicated by the frequent substitution of Telugu terms. The noun forms of some Telugu adjectives end in -ana.

Examples:

paccana	'green
pullana	'sour'
tīyana	'sweet'

Thus, in many cases, what appears to be a Koya adjectival form turns out to be a Telugu noun replacing a Koya noun. In such cases these 'adjectives' are analyzable as compound nouns rather than adjective plus noun. Similarly, the Koya nominalizing suffix -ṭi becomes confused with the Telugu adjective suffix -ti in such words as tīyati, errati, etc. Since there are no formal criteria for determining occurrence with or without adjectival suffixes, these items are included here rather than under complex adjectives.

3.75. Complex adjectives. Complex adjectives consist of verbal adjectives and derivative adjectives. Complex adjectives are formed by adding adjectival suffixes to the noun or verb stem. Verbal adjectives are discussed in 4.6.

Derivative adjectives are derived from nouns by the following suffixes: -ana ~ -anna, -atta, -al, -ti, -a, -i, -la.

-ana ~ -anna. In addition to nalla 'black', erra 'red', tella 'white', tiyya 'sweet', pulla 'sour' (3.73) -ana transforms the following nouns to adjectives:

pacca: paccana	'green'
rūci: rūcanna	'tasty'
iṣṭam: iṣṭamanna	'pleasant'
andam: andamanna	'beautiful'
balamu: balamanna	'strong'

When suffixed to words denoting 'much' (3.73) -ana functions as an 'indefinitizer'.

beckanna	'however much'

In one case -ana occurs suffixed to a verb root: rās- 'write', rāsana 'writing table'.

-atta. Except for color terms and the words for sour, sweet, and tasty, -atta occurs as the more frequent suffix for all other nouns which take -ana.

andamatta	'beautiful'
iṣṭamatta	'pleasant'
balamatta	'strong'

It is the normal suffix for nouns borrowed from Sanskrit. -atta is itself probably derived from the past adjective form of -āy 'to become', and -ana is probably an archaic form of the same verbal adjective.

-al(a). This suffix denotes belonging to what the noun denotes. It occurs most frequently with names for exogamous divisions.

maṭṭala	'of the maṭṭas'

There is some difficulty here, since -al may simply be a reduced form of -āl, the derivative suffix denoting rational males. The actual adjective suffix thus being -a. This is highly probable, since there tends to be some variation between -āl(a) and -al(a).

-ti. This suffix occurs as an adjectival suffix with Telugu loan words. It could alternatively be analyzed as oblique -t plus genitive -i. It occurs frequently only with the following:

ninne:ninneti	'yesterday'
penku: penkiti	'tile'

erra: errati	'red'
tīya: tīyati	'sweet'
pacca: paccati	'green'
cakkana: cakkati	'pretty'
nalla: nallati	'black'
pulla: pullati	'sour'
tella: tellati	'white'

-a. See the genitive case (3.43).

-i. See the genitive case (3.43).

-la. Denotes of or pertaining to that denoted by the noun stem. It is most frequently used with the numeral one hundred and with Telugu loan words.

āyḍu vandala lēyōru 'five hundred youths'

This is the Telugu form and it varies freely with the regular Koya genitival construction.

āyḍu vandāni lēyōru 'five hundred youths'

3.76. Monomorphemic adverbs. Monomorphemic adverbs consist of words unanalyzable into constituent morphemes. These include adverbs of time, place, and manner.

Adverbs of time:

beske	'when'
aske	'then'
inje	'now'
nāḍi	'tomorrow'
ninne	'yesterday'
onne	'day before yesterday'
nēṇḍu	'day, today'

The first three items have allomorphs of the demonstrative adjectives ā-, ī-, ē- (bē-) as initial components, but since -ske or -cke and -nje do not appear to be derived from any known noun stem, they are included here. All forms denoting days seem to be derivable from nēṇḍu 'today'. There is a common stem -ne ~ -nē which appears to be prefixed by some adjectival form of the numerals.

Adverbs of place:

begge	'where'
agga ~ agge	'there'
igge	'here'

These are probably derivatives of kēṭu 'place'.

Adverbs of manner:

bēke	'which way'
āke	'that way'
īke	'this way'

bēlā	'in what manner'
ālā	'in that manner'
īlā	'in this manner'

All of these are apparently derivative, but the sources of their derivation, other than the demonstrative adjectives, are unknown.

Other monomorphemic adverbs are the following:

inka	'still, yet'
malli	'again'
mari	'again, another, then'
bāgā	'well'
sēna	'very'
vēre	'separately'
mālāwu	'loudly, greatly, excessively'
bāri	'why'
bāta	'what'

mālāwu is derivative (mā + lāwu). lāwu denotes 'great, fat, wide'. Since the initial constituent (mā) is unproductive, mālāwu is included with monomorphemic adverbs.

bāta has an allomorph bātā before the nominalizing suffix //TI// (3.79).

3.77. Complex adverbs. Complex adverbs consist of a noun, adjective, or verb base plus adverbial suffixes. Adverbial suffixes are -gā and -īnā. The latter is in free variation with -īnē. Only -gā occurs with adjective bases.

Examples: ST: Adj. + gā

cinnagā	'as small'
nallagā	'as black'

ST: N + gā

vadlavāṇḍugā	'as a carpenter'
pūrtigā	'completely'

ST: N + īnā

coppīnā	'at the rate of'
jeppīnē	'quickly'
jabbīnā	'badly'
paddīnā	'as a pig'

ST: V + gā

mandangā	'being, while being'
mirrangā	'running, while running'

ST: V + īnā

tungīnā	'doing, while doing'
mirrīnā	'running, while running'

Where either -gā or -īnā may occur there are no formal grounds for determining which will be used. It should be noted, however, that -gā is suffixed to one form of the infinitive while -īnā appears to be suffixed directly to the verb root. -gā is a borrowing from Telugu.

3.78. Expansion of qualifiers. Qualifiers differ from nouns and verbs by the fact that they can only be expanded by another member of the same form class. Expansions may be either reduplicative or cumulative. Reduplication serves to intensify the original meaning of the word. Cumulative expansion merely adds further qualifiers, thus modifying previous qualifiers.

Cumulative expansion of adverbs is limited to combinations of the monomorphemic adverbs bāgā 'well' and vēre 'separately' preceded by sēna 'very'.

sēna bāga	'very well'

Two way combinations with sēna may also occur with semantically appropriate complex adverbs.

sēna paddīna	'very like a pig'

Cumulative expansions of adjectives may consist of any semantically appropriate sequence of adjectives. The maximum elicited was the following four way expansion:

ī beriya mukemanna kaṣṭamanna pustakam	'this big, important, difficult book'

Adjectives may further be expanded by combinations with sēna and bāga as initial members.

sēna menci pustakam	'very good book'

Reduplicative expansion of adjectives consists of the repetition of the same word.

menci menci pustakam	'an excellent book'

Demonstrative adjectives cannot be expanded by reduplication. Reduplication of adverbs is similar to that of adjectives but has the added feature of balancing two adverbs differing only in their demonstrative adjectives.

askeṭiki beskeṭiki	'now and then'
aggeṭiki beggeṭiki	'here and there'
īke āke	'this way and that'

3.79. Nominalizations. All qualitative adjectives, possessive pronouns, the verbal adjective //A// (cf. 5.5), adverbs of time and place (with the exception of nāḍi), numerals (cf. 3.54) and the question word 'what' (bāta) may be converted to nouns by the suffix //TI//. //TI// has allomorphs /ṭi/, /ṭ/, /di/. /ṭi/ occurs after numerals, qualitative adjectives, and adverbs of time and place. /ṭ/ occurs after postpositions. /di/ occurs elsewhere.

Examples:

tiyya	'sweet'	tiyyaṭi	'sweet thing'
erra	'red'	erraṭi	'red thing'
pulla	'sour'	pullaṭi	'sour thing'
nēṇḍu	'day'	nēnṭi	'day it'
ninne	'yesterday'	ninneṭi	'yesterday it'

bāta	'what'	bātādi	'what it'
tungta	'do' (past V. adj)	tungtādi	'fact of doing'
nā	'my'	nādi	'my it, mine'

Possessive pronouns may also be nominalized by the suffix /vi/ denoting plurality.

nāvi	'my things' (cf. 5.5 NPH)

For numerals, qualitative adjectives and adverbs of time and place //TI// also functions as the oblique stem to which the dative case suffix or postpositions may be suffixed.

Examples:

orṛo	'one'	orrōṭiki	'for one'
nēṇḍu	'today'	nēnṭiki	'for today'
beske	'when'	besketiki	'for when'
agga	'there'	aggaṭkasi	'from there'

In general, //TI// functions like any other pronominal ending, and in fact both //TI// and /vi/ are allomorphs of the feminine/neuter pronouns (cf. 3.56). Consequently, they will hereafter be treated as nouns similar to those of class three (3.53).

3.80. Minor form classes. There are four minor form classes: clitics (Cl), interjections (In), connectives (Con), and fillers (Fi).

Clitics. Strictly interpreted, clitics are a class of suffixes, but are included here for convenience. The clitics are -ē, -ā, -ō. Suffixed to a noun, verb, adjective and some adverbs these denote emphasis, interrogation, and dubiety respectively.

Examples:

lōnē	'indeed a house'
paddē	'indeed a pig'
baṇḍā	'a cart?'
paṇḍō	'perhaps a fruit'

With personal pronouns, ē in addition to emphasis may denote reflexivity.

nannē	'I myself'

After stems in long vowels clitics have allomorphs -nē, -nā, -nō.

īlānē	'in just this way'

Interjections: Seven words occur utterance initially or in isolation as exclamations:

ān	'yes'
cītam	'yes'
ayyo	'alas'
pāpam	'pity'
cī	an expression of aversion or disgust
ehe	'fie'
abbē, abbō	exclamations denoting surprise

One word occurs phrase, clause, or sentence finally as a corroborative interrogative:

gadā	'isn't it so', 'as you know'

Connectives. Five words occur connecting phrases or predications:

ganaka	'therefore'
gōni	'but'
ginna	'also'
ika	'then'
kudā	'also, and'

kudā 'also, and' and length on the final vowel of the dative occur connecting parallel case forms. The latter denotes 'and' or 'between'.

dīnikī dānikī tēda bātādi? 'between this and that what difference'

kudā occurs after the two nouns being connected.

sīta rāmuḍu kudā 'sīta and rāma'

Fillers. Aside from hesitation phenomena, there are numerous 'fillers' occurring particularly in songs, chants, and recitations.

hē	occurs before commencing a recitation
rāyō rē rē nā	occurs at the beginning and between song verses
yammā	occurs at the end of verses, or at the end of predications within verses
kāsi	occurs after the names of goddesses in prayers, chants, and recitations.

Chapter IV

VERBS

4.1. A verb (V) consists of a nucleus ("base") plus or minus suffixes. The base may be either monomorphemic or analyzable into a root plus one or more derivational suffixes. Suffixes include tense-mode and personal ending suffixes.

On the basis of suffix distribution and syntactic position, verbs are either finite or nonfinite.

Finite verbs consist of a verbal base plus tense-mode suffixes and plus or minus personal ending suffixes. Finite verbs occur only before /./. Nonfinite verbs occur only before nonfinal junctures and do not occur with personal ending suffixes. In a formula, the verb may be represented as follows:

$$\text{Base} \qquad (+\ \text{tense-mode}) \qquad + \begin{cases}\text{non-finite suffix}\\ \text{personal ending}\end{cases}$$

4.2. The shapes of verbal bases.

Monosyllables:	Examples
V̄	ī 'give', ō 'bring'
VC	ut 'rend'
V̄C	īk 'tear'
CVC	dus 'strip', mis 'hide'
CV̄C	lāg 'pull', dēv 'dig'
V̄NC	ūng 'swing', āng 'stop'
CVNC	tung 'do', paṇḍ 'ripen'
CV̄NC	lēng 'untie', tōṇḍ 'curdle'
VNC	unj 'sleep'
CVCC	turs 'push', gebb 'gag'
CV̄CC	nērs 'learn', tīrs 'settle'
VCC	ett 'lift'
V̄CC	ūḍs 'transplant'
VCCC	ersk 'fan'
CVCCC	pursk 'feel for'

Disyllables	Examples
CVCVC	migal 'remain over', batak 'to live'
CVCVNC	tolang 'step aside', marang 'forget'
CVNCVC	paṇḍis 'cultivate'
CVCCVC	tuppis 'fling', tarkis 'argue'
CV̄CVC	gālis 'clear', cāpis 'abuse'

Trisyllables:	Examples
CVCCVCVC	kummaris 'discharge', capparis 'suck'
CV̄NCVCVC	kāngalis 'embrace'
CVNCV̄CVC	sampādis 'provide'

The restriction on the final six items is that final -VC is -is.

The following compound bases occur:

irvāṭ- 'throw away'	ir- 'to throw' + vāṭ- 'to put'
ceḍagoṭṭ- 'spoil'	ceda 'bad', 'rotten' + goṭṭ- (koṭṭ-) 'to strike'
jōgoṭṭ- 'pacify'	jō(ka) 'intercourse, friendship' + 'to strike'

The first is a compound of two verbal bases whereas the latter are derived from noun stems and a verbal base. All cases have an intensive meaning.

4.3. Roots and derivative suffixes. On the basis of comparison, there are numerous bases which contain similar or identical sequences of phonemes as components of non-initial segments. There are other instances in which a root occurs both with and without these sequences. These similar or identical sequences of phonemes constitute derivative suffixes. When a root occurs both with and without derivative suffixes, it is possible to assign a meaning to the suffix.

On the basis of their occurrence in contrastive pairs of bases, the following suffixes are transitive, intransitive, and causative.

Transitive:	-p
	-ip
	-pp
	-is
	-ht
	-c
	-t
	-s
	-is
Intransitive:	-g
	-k
	-ng
	-d
	-ḍ
	-nd
	-ṇḍ
	-l
Causative:	-is

Since there is no apparent principle for predicting transitivity-intransitivity on formal grounds, the data are classed in terms of the varying combinations of suffixes which may occur. The following list indicates this relationship.

Intransitives	Transitives	
no suffix	-ip-	-p-
-d-	-ip-	-p-
-g-	-ip-	-p-
-ng-	-ip-	-p-
-yi-		-p-
-s-		-p-
-is-	-ip-	
-ṇ-		-pp-
no suffix	-ht-	
-ḍḍ-	-ht-	
-d-	-ht-	
-tt-	-ht-	
-l-	-ht-	
-p-	-ht-	
-ng-	-ht-	
-nd-	-ht-	
-ṇḍ-	-ht-	
	-s-	
-ang-	-s-	
-g-	-c-	
-ng-	-k-	

The following list gives the pairs on which this analysis is based.

Intransitive - no suffix: transitive -p-, three sets

tē- 'bring'	tep- 'to make bring'
rāl- 'roll'	rālp- 'to make grains roll out by rubbing'
ī- 'give'	īp- 'to make give'

Intransitive - no suffix: transitive -ip-, two sets

tar- 'climb'	tarip- 'to make climb'
kuḍ- 'gather'	kuḍip- 'assemble'

Intransitive -l-: transitive -ip-, one set

nill[1]	nillip- 'to make stand'

Intransitive -d-: transitive -p-, two sets

naḍad- 'walk'	naḍap- 'to make walk'
kud- 'sit'	kup- 'to seat'

Intransitive -d-: transitive -ip-, one set

verd- 'fear'	verip- 'to frighten'

Intransitive -g-: transitive -p-, one set

dig- 'get down'	dip- 'to take down'

[1]Contrast with nikk- 'become erect', niht- 'to erect'.

Intransitive -ng-: transitive -p-, three sets

kāng- 'boil'	kāp- 'to make boil'
āng- 'stop'	āp- 'to make stop'
dāng- 'hide'	dāp- 'thrust a knife or spear into'

Intransitive -yi-: transitive -p-, three sets

teliyi- 'know'	telip- 'to make know'
kaliyi- 'meet'	kalip- 'join, mix, have intercourse'
kaḍiyi- 'rot'	kaḍip- 'to make rot'

Intransitive -s-: transitive -p-, one set

nērs- 'learn'	nērp- 'to teach'

Intransitive -is-: transitive -ip-, two sets

talis- 'to remember'	talip- 'to ask'
viḍis 'to make release'	viḍip- 'to release' (tr.)

Intransitive -ṇ-: transitive -pp-, one set

uṇṇ- 'drink'	upp- 'to make drink, to water an animal'

Intransitive - no suffix: transitive -ht-, three sets

um- 'wipe'	uht- 'to wipe' (tr.)
mēy- 'graze'	mēht- 'to make graze'
vēy- 'fry in oil'	vaht- 'to make fry in oil'

Intransitive -ḍḍ-: transitive -ht-, one set

uḍḍ- 'return, turn about'	uht- 'to make turn'

Intransitive -d-: transitive -ht, one set

tēd- 'arise'	tēht- 'to make rise'

Intransitive -tt-: transitive -ht-, two sets

pitt- 'fart'	piht- 'to blow out'
katt- 'cut'	kaht- 'to make cut'

Intransitive -l-: transitive -ht-, one set

nill- 'stand'	niht- 'to erect, make stand'

Intransitive -p-: transitive -ht-, one set

tōp- 'appear'	tōht- 'to make appear'

Intransitive -ng-: transitive -ht-, two sets

ūng- 'swing'	ūht- 'to make swing'
lēng- 'untie'	lēht- 'open'

Intransitive -nd-: transitive -ht-, one set

nind- 'become full'	niht- 'to fill'

Intransitive -ṇḍ-: transitive -ht-, two sets

nāṇḍ- 'be wet'	nāht- 'dampen'
ēṇḍ- 'dance'	ēht- 'to make dance'

Intransitive -nd-: transitive -s-, one set

māṇḍ- 'to be burnt'	mās- 'to kindle a fire'

Intransitive -ang-: transitive -s-, one set

marang- 'to become changed'	mars- 'to make change'

Intransitive -g-: transitive -c-, one set

vang- 'to bend over'	vanc- 'to make bend'

Intransitive -ng-: transitive -k-, one set

dāng- 'to hide'	dāk- 'to secure, secrete'

Most transitives in -p- or -ip-, and one case of transitive in -s-, form causatives by the addition of -is- to the transitive stem.

Examples:

Intransitive	Transitive	Causative
māṇḍ- 'be burnt'	mās 'to kindle'	māsis- 'to make kindle'
naḍad- 'to walk'	naḍap- 'make walk'	naḍapis 'make walk'
nill- 'stand'	nillip- 'make stand'	nillipis- 'make stand'
uṇṇ- 'drink'	upp- 'make drink'	uppis- 'make drink'
verd- 'fear'	verip- 'frighten'	veripis- 'to make fear'

Transitive stems in -ht- do not receive the suffix -is- unless there is no distinction between transitive and intransitive stems, i.e., an alternate form without the suffix -ht- does not occur. The causative is added to the intransitive allomorph. This parallels the usage in other bases where no distinction between transitive-intransitive stems has been recorded. The causative suffix is simply added to the infinitive allomorph of the verbal base.

Examples:

Intransitive	Transitive	Causative
tōp- 'appear'	tōht- 'make appear'	tōpis- 'make appear'
uḍḍ- 'return, turn about'	uht- 'make turn'	uḍḍis- 'make turn'
nind- 'fill'	niht- 'make fill'	nindis- 'make fill'
toht- 'bind'		tohtis- 'make bind'
deht- 'pluck'		dehtis- 'make pluck'
ass- 'buy'		assis- 'make buy'
tung- 'do'		tungis- 'make do'
muṭṭ- 'touch'		muṭṭis- 'make touch'
ūḍ- 'see'		ūḍis- 'make see'

In many cases, -is- is neither a transitive nor a causative suffix. It is commonly suffixed to abstract Sanskrit nouns as a means of transforming them into verbs.

Examples:

Noun Form	Verb Form
sōdana 'temptation'	sōdis- 'to tempt'
āsa 'desire'	āsis- 'to desire'

It is less frequently used in the same manner with native nouns.

Example:

paṇḍi 'fruit'	paṇḍis- 'to cultivate'

The derivative suffixes for which it is not possible to establish meaning appear to function like -is- in the formation of verbs derived from nouns. The suffixes are: d, al, s, c, ng, ak, k, sk, (i)yi. The following are the pairs on which this analysis is based.

Noun Form	Verb Form
-d-	
verri 'crazy'	verd- 'fear'
cīmu 'mucus'	cīd- 'to blow the nose'
bīṭa 'a crack'	viḍ- 'to separate'
pūngāri 'a flower'	pūyd- 'to bloom'
-al-	
migata 'remaining'	migal- 'to remain over'
taggu 'touch'	tagal- 'to come in contact'
ankaṇam 'open space'	āvalis- 'to yawn'
kavvu 'a snigger'	kavvalis- 'to laugh'
-s-	
tirmānam 'settlement'	tīrs- 'to settle'
tēra 'cloth netting'	tērs- 'to filter'
kolta 'a measure'	kols- 'to measure'
kū 'a shout'	kus- 'to sing as a bird'
ēti 'winnowing fan'	ēs- 'to winnow'
-c-	
muṭa 'a bag'	muc 'to close, cover'
bīṭa 'a crack'	vic- 'to crack, break'
pangāl 'a fork'	panc- 'to share, divide'
-ng-	
mula- 'a groan'	mulang- 'to groan'
gonta 'throat'	guṇang- 'to grumble'
kāka 'heat of sun'	kāng- 'to boil'
uyyal 'cradle, swing'	ūng- 'to swing'

Noun Form		Verb Form
	-ak-	
kōru 'tusk'		korak- 'to gnaw'
kellu 'hair'		kelak- 'to wind, twist'
eddi 'heat, fever'		eṇak- 'to dry up'
cāvu 'death'		avak- 'to kill'

The derivative suffix -ng- or -ang- occurs in three cases as a verb formative suffixed to a verbal root.

Form One		Form Two
	-ng-	
nill- 'to stand'		nīlang- 'to walk erect'
mars- 'to change'		marang- 'to forget'
tōl- 'to drive, lead an animal'		tolang- 'to step aside'
	-k-	
nālke 'tongue		nāk- 'to lick'
gorru 'finger nail'		gōk- 'to scratch'
	-sk-	
nulaka 'cot string'		nalask- 'to rub as in making twine or string'
erra 'red'		ersk- 'to fan coals'
	-iy-	
tirmānam 'settlement'		tiriy- 'to discuss'

4.4. Finite verbs (Vf). Deriving from the distribution of tense-mode and personal ending substitution classes, finite verbs are arranged in two structural types: (I) Base + personal ending, (II) Base + tense-mode + personal ending. The following paradigm of the finite verb tung- 'to do, make' is given under the two structural types.

I. Base + personal ending.

1. Imperative: sg. -a
   pl. -āṭi

tung-a	'do'
tung-āṭi	'please do'

II. Base + tense-mode + personal ending.

2. Non-past: -it-

tung-it-ana	'I (habitually or shall) do'
tung-it-āma	'we (incl.) habitually or shall) do'
tung-it-īni	'you (sg.) (habitually or shall) do'
tung-it-īri	'you (pl.) (habitually or shall) do'

tung-it-ōṇḍu	'he (habitually or shall) do'
tung-it-e	'she/it (habitually or shall) do'
tung-it-ōru	'they (masc.) (habitually or shall) do'
tung-it-āku	'they (fem./n.) (habitually or shall) do'
tung-it-āḍa	'we (excl.) (habitually or shall) do'

3. Past: -t-

tung-t-āna	'I did'
tung-t-āma	'we (incl.) did'
tung-t-īni	'you (sg.) did'
tung-t-īri	'you (pl.) did'
tung-t-ōṇḍu	'he did'
tung-t-ōru	'they (masc.) did'
tung-t-e	'she/it did'
tung-t-āku	'they (fem./n.) did'
tung-t-āḍa	'we (excl.) did'

4. Non-past negative: -ō-[2]

(tung-ō-āna)[3]	/tungōna/	'I (habitually or shall) not do'
(tung-ō-āma)	/tungōma/	'we (incl.) (habitually or shall) not do'
(tung-ō-īni)	/tungīni/	'you (sg.) (habitually or shall) not do'
(tung-ō-īri)	/tungīri/	'you (pl.) (habitually or shall) not do'
(tung-ō-ōṇḍu)	/tungōṇḍu/	'he (habitually or shall) not do'
(tung-ō-e)	/tungō/	'she/it (habitually or shall) not do'
(tung-ō-ōru)	/tungōru/	'they (masc.) (habitually or shall) not do'
(tung-ō-āku)	/tungōku/	'they (fem./n.) (habitually or shall) not do'
(tung-ō-āḍa)	/tungōḍa/	'we (excl.) (habitually or shall) not do'

5. Potential: -ak-[4]

(tung-ak-āna)	/tungkōnu/	'I (might) do'
(tung-ak-āma)	/tungkōma/	'we (incl.) might do'
(tung-ak-īni)	/tungkīni/	'you (sg.) might do'
(tung-ak-īri)	/tungkīri/	'you (pl.) might do'
(tung-ak-ōṇḍu)	/tungkōṇḍu/	'he might do'
(tung-ak-e)	/tungke/	'she/it might do'
(tung-ak-ōru)	/tungkōru/	'they (masc.) might do'
(tung-ak-āku)	/tungkāku/	'they (fem./n.) might do'
(tung-ak-āḍa)	/tungkāḍa/	'we (excl.) might do'

---

[2] In rapid speech and/or when the subject is understood or given, the negative may fall into a different structural type. All personal endings are dropped and the base occurs only with the tense-mode suffix -ō-. It is partially for this reason that the tense-mode sign of the negative is taken as -ō- and not as ϕ, even though all the personal endings beginning in ā have allomorphs beginning in ϕ in the future indefinite.

[3] (tung-ō-āna), etc. is morphonemic writing. Phonemically it is /tungōna/.

[4] This tense is rarely used. In its place, the non-past is used. The first person plural exclusive serves as a hortative.

6. Negative imperative: -m-

tung-m-a	'you (sg.) don't do'
tung-m-āṭi	'you (pl.) don't do'

4.5. Non-finite verbs (Vnf). Non-finite verbs fall into two structural types. (I) Base + suffix, (II) Base + tense-mode + suffix.

I. Base + Suffix.

1. present participle	-ōre	tung-ōre 'while doing'
2. Past participle	-i	tung-i 'having done'
3. Habitual adjective	-āni	tung-āni 'which does'
4. Gerund	-aṭam	tung-aṭam 'the doing'
5. Infinitive	-a	tung-a 'to do'

II. Base + tense-mode + suffix. These constructions are based either on the past tense or negative stem plus the adjective or participle suffix.

6. Adjective	-a	
(a) past adjective		tung-t-a 'which did'
(b) negative adjective		(tung-ō-a) /tungova/ 'which did not do'
7. Conditional	-ku	
(a) positive conditional		tung-t-ku 'if do'
(b) negative conditional		(tung-ō-ku) /tungūku/ 'if not do'
8. Concessive	-kanna	
(a) positive concessive		tung-t-kanna 'even though do'
(b) negative concessive		(tung-ō-kanna) /tungokanna/ 'even though not do'
9. Negative participle	-vake	(tung-ō-vāke) /tungovāke/ 'not having done'

4.6. Tense-mode suffixes. Allomorphs, distribution, and meaning of tense-mode suffixes are given in the following section.

1. The non-past //IT// refers to habitual or unrestricted future time. It occurs before personal ending suffixes. //IT// has allomorphs /-īt/, /-t/, and /-it/. /-īt/ occurs before the third singular feminine/neuter personal ending. /-t/ occurs after verbal bases in (C)Vnn or (C)Vṇṇ. (-it/ occurs elsewhere.

Examples:

	//ēnd īt E// (ēnd īt e) /ēndīte/	'she, it will dance'
	//tinn IT ANA// (tin t āna) /tintāna/	'I will eat'
	//dā˘ IT ONDU// (dā˘ it ōṇḍu) /dāyitōṇḍu/	'he will go'

2. The past //TT// expresses an action performed in past time. It occurs before personal endings, the adjective, conditional, and concessive suffixes. //TT// has allomorphs /-tt/, and /-t/. /-tt/ occurs after stems ending in (C)Vnn, (C)Vṇṇ and (C)V̄. /-t/ occurs elsewhere.

Examples:	//tinn TT ONDU//	'he ate'
	(ti tt ōṇḍu)	
	/tittōṇḍu/	
	//vāX tt ōṇḍu//	'he came'
	(vāX tt ōṇḍu)	
	/vattōṇḍu/	
	//ēs TT ORU//	'they winnowed'
	(ēs t ōru)	
	/ēstōru/	

3. The non-past negative //O// denotes negation of habitual or future action. It occurs before personal ending suffixes, the adjective, conditional, concessive, and participial suffixes. //O// has allomorphs /-ϕ/, /-v/, /-vō/, /-ū/, /-vū/, /-o/, /-ō/. /-ϕ/ occurs before the second person singular and plural personal endings, and after the defective verb VALAS when personal ending suffixes occur. /-v-/ occurs before the adjective suffix with bases in -ad or when the adjective is followed by a noun or pronoun beginning in a long back vowel. In rapid speech it frequently varies freely with /-o/. /-vō/ occurs after stems ending in -ht, -rd, and -ad unless it is followed by the adjective suffix. /-ū/ occurs before the conditional except after bases in -ht, -rd, and -ad. /-vū/ occurs after bases in -ht, -rd, and -ad. /-o/ occurs before all other non-finite suffixes. /-ō/ occurs elsewhere. It is difficult to determine whether or not there are two negative suffixes: //-u// and //-o// with respective allomorphs. The allomorph /-o/, for example, frequently seemed to be phonetically [-u], but I interpret this as the allophone [ɷ̂] occurring before back vowels (cf. 2.4).

Examples:	//vā O ORU//	'they won't come'
	(varr ō ru)	
	/varrōru/	
	//utak@O IRI//	'you (polite) won't wash'
	(utak@ ϕ īri)	
	/utikīri/	
	//ūḍ O INI//	'you won't see'
	(ūḍ ϕ īni)	
	/ūḍīni/	
	//naḍad O ANA//	'I won't walk'
	(naḍa vō na)	
	/naḍavōna/	

//dāṭ O ANA// (dāṭ ō na) /dāṭōna/	'I won't cross'
//lumm O E// (lumm ō ϕ) /lummō/	'it won't root'
//āˇ O A´ + ōṇḍu// (āˇ va´ ōṇḍu) /āyvōṇḍu/	'the one who did not become'

4. The potential //AK// has an optative-hortative connotation. It occurs before personal ending suffixes, and has allomorphs /-k/ and /-ak/. /-k/ occurs after stems ending in -k or -g. /-ak/ occurs elsewhere.

Examples:	//tung AK ANA// (tung k ōnu) /tungkōnu/	'I might do'
	//īkX AK AMA// (īkX k ōmu) /ikkōmu/	'we might tear'
	//ā AK@IRI// (ād ak@īri) /ādikīri/	'you (formal) might become'

//AK// is probably somehow related to the infinitive //AKA//. Historically, it may have been a separate "future" tense.

5. The negative imperative //M// denotes a prohibitive command. It occurs before a special set of imperative personal endings. Its allomorph is /-m/.

Examples:	//naḍad M AA// (naḍa m ā) /naḍamā/	'you (sing.) don't walk'
	//ī M AATI// (ī m āṭi) /īmāṭi/	'you (pl.) don't give'

6. The present participle //CORE// usually denotes an action occurring habitually or in present time, but its ultimate time reference is governed by the following phrase or clause. //CORE// occurs before /,/ and /+/ verb finite. It has the following allomorphs: /-jōre/, /-sōre/, /-cōre/, /-ccōre/, /-ōre/, /-ō/. /-jōre/ occurs after verb bases in (C)Vnn or (C)Vṇṇ. /-sōre/ occurs after bases in -rd, -ad, and (C)V̄ (except kē 'to tell' and tē 'to bring'). /-ccōre/ occurs after kē and tē. /-cōre/ occurs after bases ending in -ht. /-ō/ occurs only in bound constructions before the verb minn- or mann (cf. 4.10). /-ōre/ occurs elsewhere.

Examples:

//inn CORE// (in jōre) /injōre/	'while saying, so saying'
//naḍad CORE// (naḍa sōre) /naḍasōre/	'while walking'
//vā CORE// (vā sōre) /vāsōre/	'while coming'
//ēht CORE// (ēht cōre) /ēhtcōre/	'while making dance'
//kēXCORE// (kēXccore) /keccōre/	'while telling, so telling'
//sampādis CORE// (sampādis ōre) /sampādisōre/	'while earning'

7. The past participle //CI// denotes a completed past action and serves as a phrase copula. It occurs before /, /, and /+/ verb finite. Its allomorphs are: /-ji/, /-si/, /-ci/, /-cci/, /-i/. /-ji/ occurs after bases in (C)Vnn or (C)Vṇṇ. /-si/ occurs after bases in -rd, -ad, and (C)$\bar{V}$ (except kē 'to tell' and tē 'to bring'). /-ci/ occurs after bases in -ht. /-cci/ occurs after kē and tē. /-i/ occurs elsewhere.

Examples:

//punn CI// (pun ji) /punji/	'having known'
//aḍad@CI// (aḍa@si) /aḍisi/	'having cried'
//ā CI// (ā si) /āsi/	'having become'
//toht CI// (toht ci) /tohtci/	'having tied'
//tē CI// (te cci) /tecci/	'having brought'
//tōṇḍ CI// (tōṇḍ i) /tōṇḍi/	'having curdled'

8. The conditional //KU// denotes an hypothetical situation or action with no time restriction other than a non-past implication. It is sometimes used in place of the present participle to denote present action. The conditional is suffixed to the past or the negative stem. When suffixed to the negative it denotes 'if not'. It has the allomorph /-ku/.

Examples: //inn TTøKU// 'if said'
(i ttøku)
/itku/

//kuht TT KU// 'if shake'
(kuh t ku)
/kuhtku/

//āXTTøKU// 'if become'
(āXttøku)
/atku/

//tinn O KU// 'if not eat'
(tinn ū ku)
/tinnūku/

//ard O KU// 'if not fall'
(ar vū ku)
/arvūku/

//āˇ O KU// 'if not become'
(āˇ vū ku)
/āyvūku/

9. The past and negative adjective //A// indicates that the noun or adverb modified has the quality or condition denoted by the verb base. //A// is suffixed to the past tense stem, or to the negative stem. When suffixed to the negative it indicates that the noun or adverb modified does not have the quality or condition denoted by the verb base. The past adjective has a past time reference. The negative adjective may be either past or non-past. The adjective suffix occurs before /+/ N, Adv, Po. It has allomorphs /-va/, /ā/ and /-a/. /-va/ occurs after the negative allomorph /-o/. /ā/ occurs before the nominalizing suffix //TI//. /-a/ occurs elsewhere.

Examples: //naḍad O A// 'which did not walk'
(naḍa v a)
/naḍava/

//dāˇ O A// 'which did not go'
(dāˇ o va)
/dāyova/

//inn TT A´ONDU// 'the one who said'
(i tt a´ ōṇḍu)
/ittōṇḍu/

//tung TT A payya//	'after doing'
(tung t a payya)	
/tungtapayya/	

Since /-a/ is elided before long vowels it is often difficult to distinguish the adjective from the simple past or negative when a pronoun or noun beginning with a long vowel follows the adjective. This is particularly true with the pronouns ōru and ōṇḍu. In rapid speech the negative adjective is collapsed after the bases ī 'to give' and ō 'to bring' when a pronoun or noun beginning with a long vowel follows the adjective.

Example:	//ī˘ O a ORU//	'They are the ones who won't, don't give'
	(ī˘ o va ōru)	
	/īvōru/ ~ /ivvōru/	

10. The habitual adjective //ANI// refers to a repetitive or habitual action in past or present time and indicates that the noun or adverb modified has the quality or condition denoted by the verbal base. It is suffixed directly to the verbal base and occurs before /+/ N, Adv, Po. It has the allomorph /-āni/.

Examples:	//kēnj ANI//	'which hears, listens'
	(kēnj āni)	
	/kēnjāni/	
	//ēnd ANI//	'which dances'
	(ēnd āni)	
	/ēndāni/	
	//tung ANI tīru//	'the method of doing'
	(tung āni tīru)	
	/tungāni tīru/	

11. The concessive //KANNA// denotes an hypothetical situation, the occurrence of which cannot alter a condition or action. It is generally equivalent to 'even though' in English. It is suffixed either to the past or negative stem. The negative is equivalent to English 'even though did not'. It occurs before /,/ and has the allomorph /-kanna/.

Examples:	//vāXTTøKANNA//	'even though come'
	(vāXttøkanna)	
	/vatkanna/	
	//mirr O KANNA//	'even though not run'
	(mirr o kanna)	
	/mirrokanna/	

/-kanna/ is actually comprised of the conditional / ku/ + anna the "indefinitizing" suffix (3.56, 3.73, 3.75).

12. The negative participle //VAKE// denotes 'without', 'not having become' whatever the verb denotes. It is suffixed to the negative stem and occurs before /,/. It has free variants /-vāke/ ~ /-vā/.

Examples: //puṭṭ O VAKE// 'not having been born'
(puṭṭ o vāke)
/puṭṭovāke/

//vā O VAKE// 'not having come'
(varr o vāke)
/varrovāke/

13. The infinitive //AN// occurs before /+/ V, /+/ N, /+/ //IN//, /+/ gā ~ īna. It has allomorphs /-a/, /-aka/, /-ana/. The meaning of the latter is more nearly that of a gerund since it only occurs before the oblique suffix in a construction restricted to the dative or before another noun. The final vowel, like regular -a ending noun declensions, is lengthened before the oblique.

Example: tunganānki 'for the doing'

There is some variation here, for /-a/ sometimes occurs before the oblique. Again, the vowel is lengthened.

Example: tungāniki 'for the doing'

/-a/ however, usually occurs only before another verb in periphrastic constructions. /-ana/ never occurs before another verb and /-a/ never occurs before a noun. /-aka/ occurs only in periphrastic constructions usually before the verb ā 'become' or ī 'give', though it infrequently occurs before other verbs as well. The verbs with which /-aka/ occurs do not overlap those with which /-a/ occurs. For description of the latter, see 4.10. /-aka/ frequently occurs in constructions which are either passive or statements of ability.

Example: /tōpakattōṇḍu/
(tōp aka āXtt ōṇḍu) 'he appeared' ('he became seeable')

/-ana/ occurs before the adverbial suffix -ga and /-a/ occurs before the adverbial suffix -īnā (3.77).

14. The gerund //ATAM//. Normally, the gerund is simply the habitual adjective plus addu, the third singular feminine/neuter pronoun.

Example: //talap&ANI ′ addu// 'the asking'
(talap&āni ′ addu)
/talapanaddu/

There is a tendency for this construction to be replaced by the Telugu gerund -aṭam.

Example: /talapaṭam/ 'the asking'

As in Telugu, this form occurs before the oblique in dative constructions. As in normal -m ending nouns, the -m is elided before the oblique and the vowel is lengthened.

Example: /talapaṭāniki/ 'for the asking'

Again, as in Telugu, -ṭ- in this suffix varies freely with -ḍ-.

Example: /talapaḍāniki/ 'for the asking'

It should be noted that this formation overlaps that of /-ana/ above. The gerund based on verbal adjective plus addu does not enter into this type of construction. It occurs only in citation forms and before another verb. //ATAM// occurs before the oblique, before another gerund, or before another verb. Sequences of more than one gerund have a copulative function.

Examples:	uṇḍaṭam māydaṭam	'drinking and fighting'
	uṇḍaṭam uṇḍaṭam	'drinking and drinking'

4.7. Personal ending suffixes (PE). Like the pronouns from which they derive, personal ending suffixes are divided into two sub-sets. (a) Those showing agreement for person and number, and (b) Those showing agreement for person, number, and gender. In addition, there is a set of imperative personal endings which is differentiated only for number. Personal endings (a) and (b) occur after tense-mode suffixes and before /./. The imperative personal endings are suffixed directly to the verbal base or the negative imperative modal suffix and occur before /./.

The imperative suffixes are: //AA// singular, //ATI// plural. Both refer only to second person. //AA// has allomorphs /-a/, / -u/, /-m/, /-mu/. /-u/ occurs after bases in (C)Vnn and (C)Vṇṇ (except mann and punn). /-m/ occurs after bases ending in -ht. /-mu occurs after ī 'give', and ō 'bring' and ā 'become'. /-a/ occurs elsewhere.

Examples: //tinn AA// 'you (sing.) eat'
(tinn u)
/tinnu/

//toht AA// 'you (sing.) tie'
/toh m)
/toh m/

//ō AA// 'you (sing.) bring'
(ō mu)
/ōmu/

//kē AA// 'you (sing.) tell'
(kell a)
/kella/

//ATI// has allomorphs /-ūṭi/, /-mūṭi/, /-āṭi/. /-ūṭi/ occurs after the verbal bases inn 'say', ann 'go', and tinn 'eat'. /-mūṭi/ occurs after bases in -ht and the verbal bases ī 'give' and ō 'bring'. /-aṭi/ occurs elsewhere.

Examples: //inn ATI// 'please say', 'you (pl.) say'
(inn ūti)
/innūṭi/

//roht ATI// 'please send', 'you (pl.) send'
(roh mūṭi)
/rohmuṭi/

//ī ATI// (ī muti) /īmūṭi/	'please give', 'you (pl.) give'
//vā ATI// (varr āṭi) /varrāṭi/	'please come', 'you (pl.) come'

The personal endings for sets a and b are as follows:

	Singular	Plural
(a) First person	//ANA//	//AMA// (exclusive) //ADA// (inclusive)
Second person	//INI//	//IRI//
(b) Third person masc.	//ONDU//	//ORU//
Third person f./n.	//E//	//AKU//

//ANA// has allomorphs /-na/, /-ōnu/, /-ϕ/, /-āna/. /-na/ occurs after the negative suffix. /-ϕ/ varies freely with /-na/. /-ōnu/ occurs after the potential suffix. /-āna/ occurs elsewhere.

//AMA// has allomorphs /-ma/, /-ōma/, /-ϕ/, /-āma/. /-ma/ occurs after the negative suffix. /-ϕ/ varies freely with /-ma/, /-ōma/ occurs after the potential suffix. /-āma/ occurs elsewhere.

//INI// has the allomorph /-īni/, /-ϕ/. /-ϕ/ varies freely with /-īni/ after the negative suffix. /-īni/ occurs elsewhere.

//IRI// has the allomorph /-īri/, /-ϕ/. /-ϕ/ varies freely with /-īri/ after the negative suffix. /īni/ occurs elsewhere.

//ADA// has allomorphs /-ōḍa/, /-ḍa/, /-ϕ/, /āḍa/. /-ōḍa/ occurs after the potential suffix. /-ḍa/ occurs after the negative suffix. /-ϕ/ varies freely with /-ḍa/. /-āḍa/ occurs elsewhere.

//E// has allomorphs /-e/, /-ϕ/, /-ϕ/ occurs after the negative suffix. /-e/ occurs elsewhere.

//AKU// has allomorphs /-ōku/, /-ku/, /-ϕ/, /-ān/, /-āku/. /-ōku/ occurs after the potential suffix. /-ku/ occurs after the negative suffix. /-ϕ/ varies freely with /-ku/. /-ān/ varies freely with /-āku/. /-āku/ occurs elsewhere.

4.8. Verb classes. Verbal bases have allomorphs before tense-mode and personal ending suffixes. Seven inflectional classes are established on the basis of this allomorphy.

Class one. No change in the stem before suffixes. This class comprises three subclasses.

(a) Monosyllabic bases in (C)V̄C, (C)VNC, (C)V̄NC, (C)VC, (C)VCC, (C)VCC
(b) Disyllabic bases in CVCVCC, CV̄CVCC, V̄CCVCC, VCCC
(c) Trisyllabic bases in CVCCV̄CVC, CV̄NCVCVC, CVCCVCVC

In all subclasses, final CC is not geminate. All consonants except -n and -y occur as final C. In bases of (C)V̄NC, final C may not be -ḍ.

Basic Stem		Stem Alternates
(a) tung-	'to do'	none
(a) dāṭ-	'to cross'	none
(b) velis-	'to shine'	none
(b) coparis-	'to sort'	none
(c) sampādis-	'to earn'	none

This is, by far, the largest single class, accounting for roughly 65 percent of all verbal bases.

Class two. The final consonant is lost before the negative, the past, the negative imperative, the present and past participial suffixes. This class consists of two subclasses.

(a) Monosyllabic bases in (C)Vht, (C)V̄ht, (C)Vrd, CV̄rd.
(b) Disyllabic bases in (C)Vḍad.

Basic Stem		Suffix	Stem Alternates
(a) kuht-	'to shake'	/TT, O, M, CORE, CI//	kuh-
(a) ard-	'to fall'	/TT, O, M, CORE, CI//	ar-
(a) ēht-	'make dance'	/TT, O, M, CORE, CI//	ēh-
(a) pārd-	'to sing'	/TT, O, M, CORE, CI//	pār-
(b) naḍad-	'to walk'	/TT, O, M, CORE, CI//	naḍa-
(b) aḍad-	'to cry'	/TT, O, M, CORE, CI//	aḍa-

Class three. This class consists of disyllabic bases in (C)VCV_2C, (C)V̄CV_2C, CVCV_2NC, CVNCV_2C, where V_2 is a. In this class V_2 is harmonic with vowels in the following suffix: (A) Before suffixes with front vowels V_2 is i, (B) before suffixes containing o (short or long) V_2 is a, and (C) before u or ū V_2 is u (cf. 2.25).

Basic Stem		Stem Alternates before Suffix Class		
		(A)	(B)	(C)
korak	'to gnaw'	korik-	korak-	koruk-
vāṇak	'to tremble'	vaṇik-	vaṇak-	vāṇuk-
tolang	'to step aside'	toling-	tolang-	tolung-
utak	'to wash'	utik-	utak-	utuk-

Class four. This class consists of six monosyllabic bases in (C)Vnn and (C)Vṇṇ. Bases have allomorphs in:

(A) (C)VC before the non-past, the negative imperative, and the present and past participial suffixes.

(B) (C)V before the past tense suffix.

(C) CVnd, CVṇd before the imperative personal endings, the habitual adjective suffix, the infinitive, and the potential.

Basic Stem		Stem Alternate before Suffix (A)	(B)	(C)
inn	'to say'	in-	i-	ind-
tiṇṇ	'to eat'	tin-	ti-	tind-
uṇṇ	'to drink'	uṇ-	u-	uṇḍ-
punn	'to know'	pun-	pu-	pund-
kann	'to give birth'	kan-	ka-	kand-
mann	'to be'	man-	ma-	mand-

inn and tinn have variant forms in the imperative: inn- and tinn-. mann has suppletive forms (4.9). ann, the allomorph of dā ('to go') and the defective verb konn (4.9) belong to this class.

Class five. This class is composed of monosyllabic bases in (C)VCC where final CC may be any geminated consonant. These bases have allomorphs before the past tense and the negative imperative suffixes. The final consonant is dropped before these suffixes (cf. 2.28).

Basic Stem		Stem Alternate before Suffix	
ett	'to lift'	/TT, M//	et-
pokk	'to blister'	/TT, M//	pok-
lumm	'to root'	/TT, M//	lum-
kicc	'to pinch'	/TT, M//	kic-
gebb	'to stuff'	/TT, M//	geb-
rudd	'to rub'	/TT, M//	ruḍ-
puṭṭ	'be born'	/TT, M//	puṭ-
dipp	'to take down'	/TT, M//	dip-
pann	'to conspire'	/TT, M//	pan-
givv	'to scratch'	/TT, M//	giv-
ḍoll	'to die'	/TT, M//	ḍol-
ogg	'to step on'	/TT, M//	og-
uḍḍ	'to return'	/TT, M//	uḍ-
ass	'to buy'	/TT, M//	as-

Class six. This class consists of two subclasses.

(a) Monosyllabic bases in CV̄Nd or CV̄Nḍ.

(b) Disyllabic bases in CVCVC where final C is y. Final C is lost before the past and negative imperative suffixes.

Basic Stem		Stem Alternate before Suffix	
(a) tōṇḍ	'to curdle'	/TT, M//	tōṇ-
nāṇḍ	'to be wet'	/TT, M//	nān-
ēnd	'to dance'	/TT, M//	ēn-
(b) teliy	'to know'	/TT, M//	teḷi-
kaḍiy	'to rot'	/TT, M//	kaḍi-
tiriy	'to discuss'	/TT, M//	tiri-

A broader analysis would merge classes five and six, and a finer analysis would segregate (a) and (b). Subclass (b) might be explained as another instance of fronting (cf. 2.24), but since the -y occurs before short vowels where -i would be expected to elide (cf. 2.21), it has been retained here as a special process.

Class seven. This class consists of nine irregular bases in (C)V̄. Since the alternates cannot be conveniently predicted on formal grounds, each base is listed separately with its alternates.

Basic Stem		Stem Alternate before Suffix						

		//IT//	//AN//
			//AK//
			//ANI//
				//TT//	//M//	//O//	//AA//
							//ATI//
								//CORE//
								//CI//

ī	'give'	īy-	īd-	i-	ī-	īv-	ī-	ī-
ō	'bring'	ōy-	ōd-	o-	ō-	ōv-	ō-	ō-
ā	'become'	āy-	ād-	a-	āy-	āy-	āy-	ā-
vā	'come'	vāy-	vād-	va-	vād-	varr-	varr-	vā-
dā	'go'	dāy-	dāy-	a-	an-	ann-	dāy-	an-
$kē_1$	'tell'	kēy-	kēt-	ke-	kel-	kēy- kell-	kell-	ke-
$kē_2$	'shout'	kēy-	kēd-	ke-	kēy-	kēy-	kēy-	kē-
vē	'boil'	vēy-	vēd-	ve-	vēy-	vēy-	vēy-	vē-
tē	'bring'	tēy-	tēd	ta-	tē-	tarr-	tarr-	ta-

Allomorphy before //IT//, //TT// and //O// with the exception of vā-, kē-, and tē- can be explained by automatic morphophonemic rules (2.24, 2.27). The final -d occurring before the infinitive, gerund, potential, and habitual adjective also occurs before these suffixes in class four. With the exception of vā, dā, and tē, bases in (C)V̄ have free variants (C)V̄v ~ (C)Vvv or (C)V̄y ~ (C)Vyy before the negative suffix.

4.9. Defective, suppletive, and auxiliary verbs.

(1) Defective verbs. There are seven defective verbs: ir 'to put', kā 'to become', mēl 'to be good', valas 'should, ought', ill 'to be not', konn 'to acquire', vaccu 'to allow'.

ir occurs only in compound form with vāṭ 'to put', irvāṭ 'to throw away'

kā occurs before -āli, the obligative form of valas, kāvāli 'it is necessary'. It also occurs in other periphrastic constructions with the defective verb valas: kāvalstakallu 'palm wine which was necessary'.

mēl occurs only in adjectival constructions in the past and negative. mēltaddu 'that which is, was good', mēlvo 'that which is, was not good'.

//VALAS// occurs only in periphrastic constructions. It has a complete conjugation in the non-past and the negative. The past tense suffix occurs only in adjectival constructions. It also forms a pluperfect with what appears to be the past participle suffix. Derived from valas is an obligative form -āli.

In its past, pluperfect, and obligative forms valas denotes "necessity" or "obligation". Elsewhere it denotes "ability" or "capacity". valas has allomorphs /ālasi/, /āls/, /āli/ /āl/. /ālasi/ occurs only in the pluperfect. /ăls/ occurs before the past tense suffix. /āli/ occurs before /./. /āl/ occurs elsewhere. In forming the negative, the personal suffix is added directly to the infinitive base without the negative suffix.

Example:

//tung AN\` VALAS IT ANA// (tunga \` āl it āna) /tungālitāna/	'I am able to do'
//tung AN\` VALAS O ANA// (tunga \` āl ϕ āna) /tungālāna/	'I am unable to do'
//tung AN \`VALAS O A ´ ONDU// (tunga \` āl o va ´ ōṇḍu) /tungālovōṇḍu/ ~ /tungālvōṇḍu/	'the one who is unable to do'
//tung AN\` VALAS TTA pani// (tunga \` āls t a pani) /tungālstapani/	'work which was necessary'
//tung AN\` VALAS// (tunga\` ālasi) /tungālasi/	'should have done'
//tung AN\` VALAS// (tunga \` āli) /tungāli/	'must do'

//ILL// is a suppletive form of mann 'to be'. It occurs in finite form without tense morphemes before the personal ending suffixes as a simple negation of existence. In periphrastic constructions it occurs before the negative suffix followed by the adjective or concessive suffixes. It also occurs independently with the negative suffix before the conditional. In this construction it is a simple connective denoting "or" and has the same distribution as other connectives. It has the allomorphs /il/, /ill/. il occurs before the negative adjective suffix when the adjective is followed by nouns beginning with long back vowels. /ill/ occurs elsewhere.

Examples:

//ILL E// (ill e) /ille/	'it, she is not'
//ILL ONDU// (ill ōṇḍu) /illōṇḍu/	'he is not'

//cadavAN´ ILL O A´ ONDU// 'the one who did not read'
(cadava´ il v a´ ōṇḍu)
/cadavilvōṇḍu/

//reṇḍu´ ILL O KU muṇḍu// 'two or three'
(rendu´ ill ū ku muṇḍu)
/reṇḍillūku muṇḍu/

Even though it usually denotes past time, ill with the negative adjective frequently occurs when the normal negative adjective would be expected. In finite constructions, ille is the most common form, the feminine/neuter suffix replacing all other personal ending suffixes.

konn occurs only in periphrastic constructions as a reflexive. It occurs only before the past and non-past tense suffixes. It occurs almost exclusively with verbs borrowed from Telugu.

Example: /cadava kontāna/ 'I will read to myself' ('I will study')

vaccu occurs only in periphrastic constructions.

Example: tinna vaccu 'he, she, it, you, etc. may eat'

In rapid speech, vaccu has a free variant occu.

Example: /tinnoccu/

With the exception of ir, ill, and mēl, these verbs are all borrowings from Telugu.

(2) Suppletive verbs. There are two suppletive verbs. ill 'not', minn 'to be'. Both are suppletive forms of mann 'to be'. For ill, see 4.10B. minn occurs in bound progressive forms (4.4) and before the third person singular feminine/neuter personal ending. Occasionally it varies freely with mann before the third person plural feminine/neuter personal ending. minn has only a single form (minn) for both past and non-past with an allomorph (mind) before the third person singular personal ending.

(3) Auxiliary verbs. There are three auxiliary verbs. kūḍadu 'ought not', voddu 'don't', kuntā 'without'. All occur in periphrastic constructions. The first two occur before /./ and the latter before /,/. voddu has a free variant oddu.

Examples: dāya kūḍadu 'ought not go'
dāya voddu ~ dāyoddu 'don't go'
dāya kuntā 'without going'

4.10. Verb expansions. Verbs may be expanded in two ways. (1) by periphrasis and (2) by prior attribute.

(1) Periphrastic constructions. Periphrastic constructions are of three structural types.

(a) Base + participle + { ī 'to give' / mann 'to be' / minn 'to be' }

(b) Base + infinitive + { par 'befall' / defective verb / auxiliary verb }

(c) Base + participle + base + infinitive + ill

(a) Base + participle + { ī / mann. / minn }

The participle may be either the present or past participle. These constructions form a future perfect, a pluperfect, a progressive future, a progressive, an imperfect, a negative imperfect, and a permissive.

The future perfect consists of base + past participle + mann + non-past suffix + personal ending suffixes (base + CI + mann + IT + PE).

Example: //vāCI mann IT ONDU// 'he will have come'
(vā si man t ōṇḍu)
/vāsimantōṇḍu/

The pluperfect is formed by base + past participle + minn + personal ending (base + CI + minn + PE).

Example: //vā CI minn E// 'she has, had come'
(vā si mind e)
/vāsiminde/

The progressive future is formed by base + present participle + mann + non-past + personal endings (base + CORE + mann + IT + PE).

Example: //pēc CORE mann IT ONDU// 'he would be starting'
(pēc ō man t ōṇḍu)
/pēcōmantōṇḍu/

The progressive is formed similarly except that minn rather than mann is used.

Example: //pēc CORE minn ANA// 'I am starting'
(pēc ō minn āna)
/pēcōminnāna/

The progressive of mann is minn.

The imperfect consists of base + present participle + mann + past tense + personal ending (base + CORE + mann + TT + PE).

Example: //cadav CORE mann TT ANA// 'I was reading'
(cadav ō ma tt āna)
/cadavōmattāna/

The imperfect may also occur with the non-finite forms of mann.

The negative imperfect is comprised of base + present participle + mann + infinitive + ill + personal ending (base + CORE + mann + AN + ILL + PE).

Example: //cadav CORE mann AN´ILL E// 'I was not studying'
(cadav ō mand a´ ill e)
/cadavōmandille/

The permissive consists of base + past participle + ī + tense + personal ending (base + CI + i + {TT / IT} + PE).

Example: //viḍad CI` ī˅ IT ANA// 'I will allow him to go' (i.e., 'I will give him release')
(viḍa si` ī˅ it āna)
/viḍisīyitāna/

(b) Base + infinitive + { par 'befall' / defective verb / auxiliary verb }

These constructions comprise a past negative, a reflexive, a permissive, an optative, a positive of ability, a negative of ability, a prohibitive, a negative optative, a negative participle, and a passive.

The past negative consists of base + infinitive + ill + personal ending (base + AN´ + ILL + E).

Example: //ō AN´ILL E// 'he, she, you, etc. did not bring'
(ōd a´ ill e)
/ōdille/

The reflexive is formed on base + infinitive + konn + tense + personal ending (base + AN + konn + IT + ANA).

Example: //kēnj AN konn IT ANA// 'I will hear for myself'
(kēnj a kon t āna)
/kēnjakontāna/

The permissive consists of base + infinitive + vaccu.

Example: //vā AN ´vaccu// 'he, she, it, etc. may come'
(vād a´ occu)
/vādoccu/

The optative consists of base + infinitive + VALAS + tense ± adjective (base + AN + VALAS + TT ± A).

Example: //tinn AN` VALAS TT A kāy// 'vegetable which should have been eaten'
(tinn a ` āls t a kāy)
/tinnālstakāy/

A positive of ability can be formed in either of two ways: (a) base + infinitive + mann + non-past + personal ending.

Example: //tarr AN mann IT ANA// 'I can climb'
(tarr a man t āna)
/tarramantāna/

(b) base + infinitive + VALAS + IT + PE.

Example: //tarr AN` āl IT ANA// 'I can climb'
(tarr a` āl it āna)
/tarrālitāna/

The negative of ability consists of base + infinitive + VALAS + negative + personal ending or adjective.

Example: //mirr AN ` VALAS O ONDU// 'he cannot run'
(mirr a` āl ϕ ōṇḍu)
/mirrālōṇḍu/

The prohibitive is formed by base + infinitive + voddu.

Example: //vā AN ´ voddu// 'don't come'
(vād a´ oddu)
/vādoddu/

The negative optative consists of base + infinitive + kūḍadu.

Example: //ūd AN kūdadu// 'one ought not see'
(ūḍ a kūḍadu)
/ūḍakūḍadu/

The negative participle consists of base + infinitive + kuntā.

Example: //ūḍs AN kuntā// 'without transplanting'
(ūḍs a kuntā)
/ūḍsakuntā/

I could discover no criterion for determining when kuntā would occur in place of the normal negative participle suffix. There appears to be no difference in meaning between the two constructions.

The passive consists of base + infinitive + par + tense ± personal ending (base + AN + par + {IT, TT, O} + PE)

Example: //ī AN par TT E// '(it) was given'
(īd a par t e)
/īdaparte/

(c) Base + infinitive + base + infinitive + ill + personal ending. This construction forms a past negative of ability. The second base is restricted to ā 'become'.

Example: //kē AN` ā AN´ILL ANA// 'I could not tell'
(kell a`ād a´ill āna)
/kellādillāna/

(2) Expansion by prior attribute. Verbs may also be expanded by adverbs occurring before the verbal base.

Example: bāgā minnōṇḍu 'he is well'
sēna lāvugā minde 'she is very fat'

4.11. Summary of verb constructions. The following flow chart summarizes verb constructions. Form classes are given in parentheses.

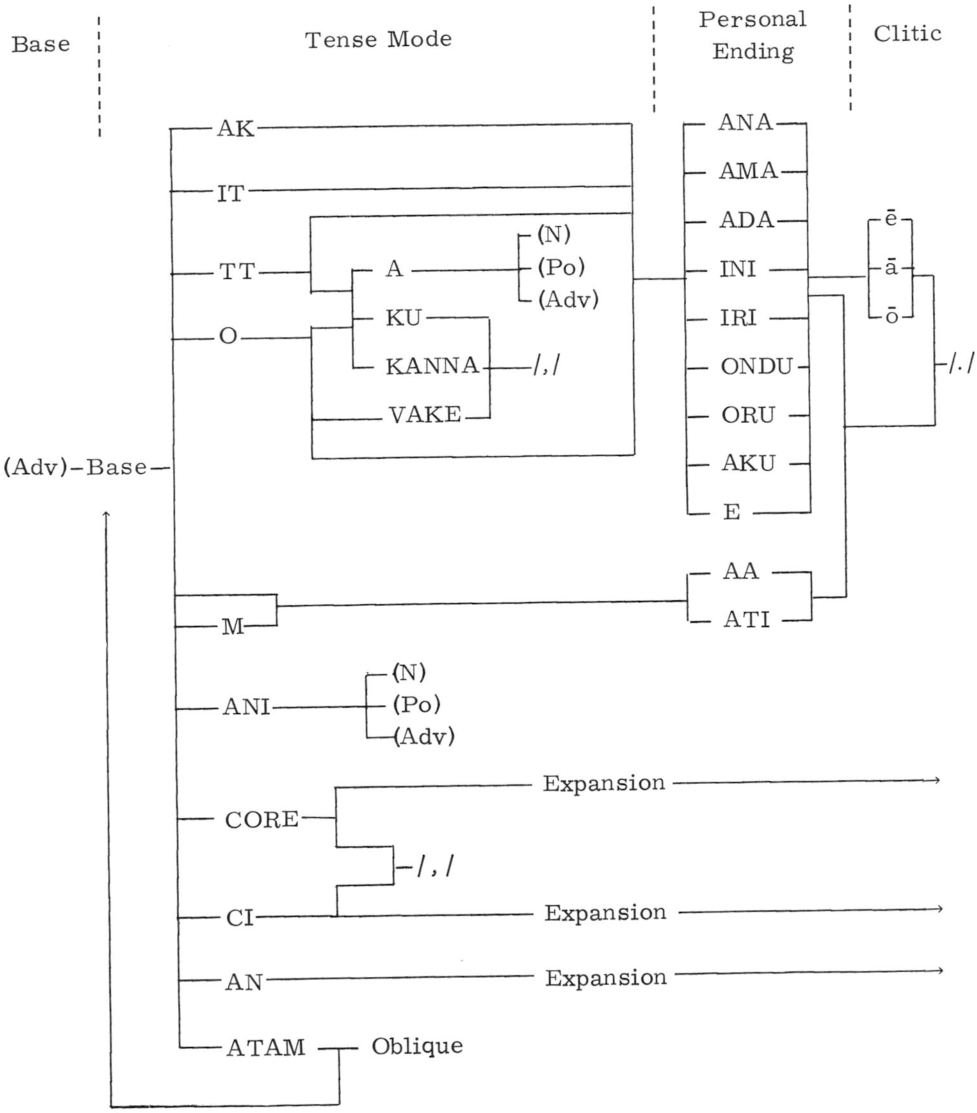

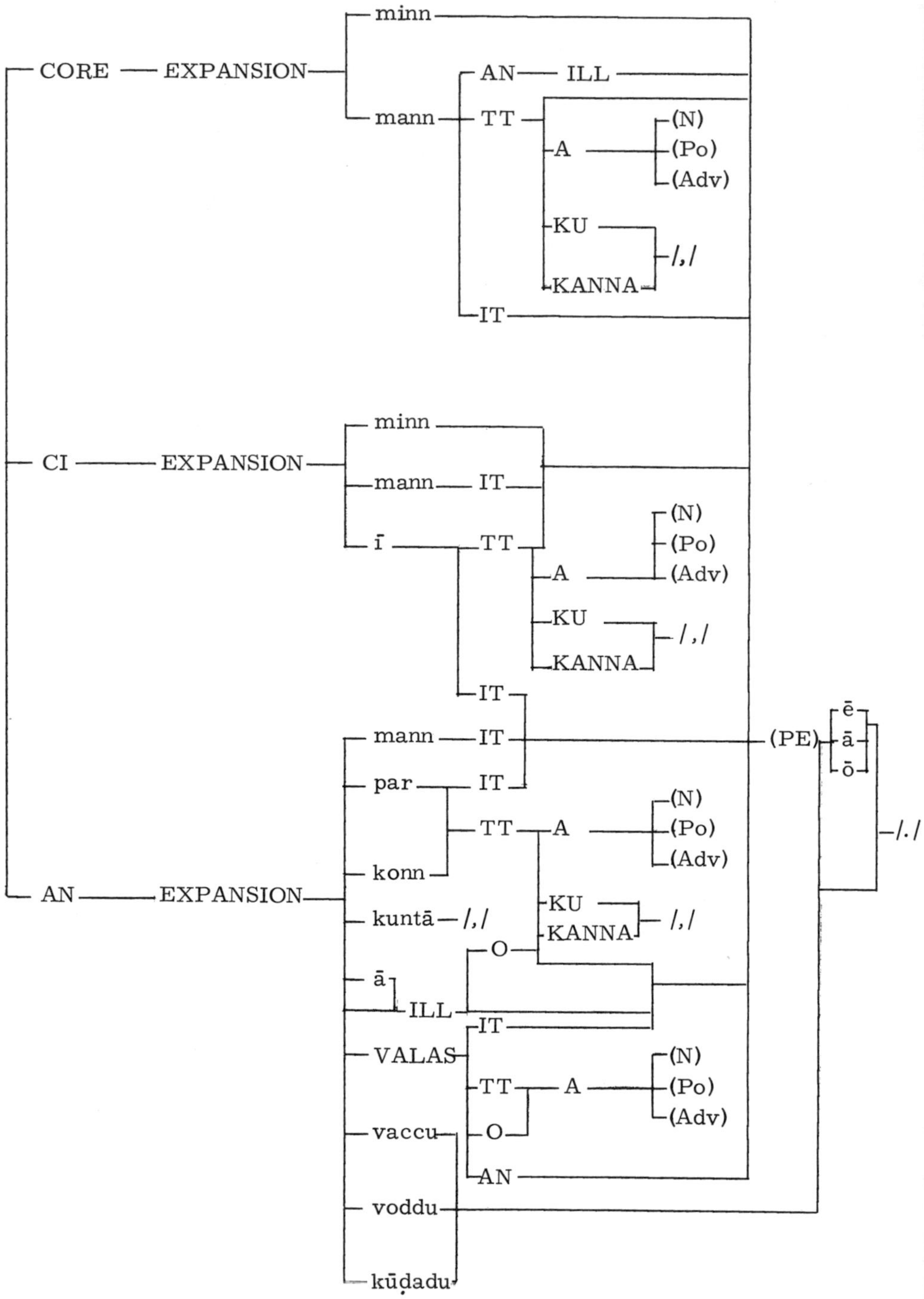
minn
CORE
EXPANSION
AN
ILL
mann
TT
(N)
A
(Po)
(Adv)
KU
/,/
KANNA
IT
minn
CI
EXPANSION
mann
IT
ī
TT
(N)
(Po)
A
(Adv)
KU
/,/
KANNA
IT
ē
mann
IT
(PE)
ā
ō
par
IT
(N)
TT
A
(Po)
/./
konn
(Adv)
AN
EXPANSION
KU
kuntā
/,/
/,/
KANNA
O
ā
ILL
IT
VALAS
(N)
TT
A
(Po)
vaccu
O
(Adv)
AN
voddu
kūḍadu

Chapter V

SYNTAX

5.1. There are seven major external distribution classes:

S	subject nouns
O	object nouns
Sc	sociative nouns
L	locative nouns
Ab	ablative nouns
Vf	finite verbs
Vnf	non-finite verbs

These are equivalent to major tactic units—nominative, dative, locative, etc., with the following exceptions. Object nouns include both the dative (O^1) and accusative (O^2) case endings. Possessive nouns are not included (see 3.72). The locative and instrumental aspects of the locative-instrumental case endings are not differentiated.

5.2. There are seven minor external distribution classes:

Cl	clitics
Ew	echo words
Po	post positions
In	interjections
Con	connectives
Fi	fillers
Tw	time words

With the exception of Tw, these are coterminous with minor form classes. Tw consists of the adverbs of time and place, and of the adverbs inka 'also, yet, still', mari 'again, another, then'. It also includes the noun or postpositions payya and perke 'after' in the constructions ā payya, ā perke 'afterwards, next'. In this class are all other nouns denoting time.

Examples:	balivina	'night, all night'
	rātri	'night'
	poḍudu	'morning'
	madyānam	'mid-day'

5.3. The classes listed in 5.1 are distributed as follows:

S. Usually initial, but may be interchanged with L and O^1. With a finite verb S as a pronoun is frequently omitted. When S occurs with a finite verb S and the personal ending of the finite verb are in congruence with each other (i.e., same person, number, and gender).

O^1. The dative frequently occurs immediately before the verb, particularly when the verb denotes motion. This is hardly determinative, however, for when the locative occurs, it will normally occur between the dative and the verb. This order also is frequently reversed.

Example: nāṭēniki baṇḍīte vattōṇḍu ~ baṇḍīte nāṭēniki vattōṇḍu

Both orders are acceptable. Similarly, when O^2 occurs, it will usually intervene between the dative and the verb, especially when the dative is suffixed to a verbal noun.

O^2. The accusative usually occurs immediately before the verb, though it is frequently supplanted by an interrogative or the locative. There are numerous cases of the direct object occurring without the accusative suffix, except when the substantive is a pronoun. Normally, the accusative suffix occurs when the verb has a transitive suffix, but even this rule is frequently violated.

Sc. The sociative has considerable freedom of occurrence, but usually occurs after the subject and before the dative. In a few instances it occurs before the subject. Positions of locative and sociative appear to be interchangeable. This is also true of the instrumental aspect of the locative-instrumental case suffix.

L. The locative normally follows the subject and may occur before or after the dative. In constructions containing an accusative, the locative occurs immediately after the accusative. There are cases of the locative occurring initially before the subject.

Ab. The ablative follows a pattern similar to the locative.

Vf. Finite verbs occur finally and can only be followed by the clitics ā, ē, ō, or by another finite verb when the two verbs are connected by quotative forms of inn 'to say'.

Vnf. Non-finite verbs occur before non-final junctures. Adjective forms of the verb are governed by rules of occurrence for the nouns or adverbs they proceed. Distribution of other forms of the verb are given in 4.6.

With the exception of postpositions and time words, the occurrence of minor distribution classes has been given (see 3.80).

Po. All postpositions usually occur with substantives following the subject. Postpositions often precede the accusative, but this is frequently reversed. In general, the distribution of postpositions is similar to that of the locative.

Tw. Time words normally occur initially, but may follow the subject. In these cases they will either occur in immediate constituency with the verb, or immediately after the subject.

These distribution classes are combined to form larger constructions—clauses, phrases, and sentences.

5.4. The clause (CL). A clause is any sequence of tactic units.

1. Preceded by /,/ or silence.
2. Followed by /,/ or /./.
3. Containing one V or containing an Adv or Po denoting time, place or manner, which is:
   (a) preceded by a verbal adjective or the infinitive
   (b) followed by /,/
4. Containing one or no S.
5. Containing no, one, two or three Po, L, Sc or Ab.
6. Containing no, one, two, three, or four O. If there are more than two O, one may be O^1 and the other O^2, or both may be O^1 or O^2.
7. Containing no, one or two Tw.

A clause containing a Vf is a CLVf, one containing a Vnf is a CLVnf, one containing an Adv is a CLAdv. The acceptable sequence of units has been given in 5.3. The following are examples of the distribution of units in the clause. All constructions are in immediate constituency with /,/ or /./.

CLVf:

Tw		Po	Vf
/malla	pēnu	mandētagga	vāyitōru./
again	god	shed near	they will go

CLVnf:

Tw	O^2	Vnf
/agge	kōrapīsēn	kōysi,/
there	chicks	having cut

CLVf:

L		L	Vf
/gōrkāte	goḍḍini	pakkāte	koṭṭitōṇḍu./
with spear	in cow's	side	he will thrust, strike

CLVf:

S	O^2	Vf
/andōru	dōḍa	tintōru./
all	cooked rice	they will eat

CLVnf:

O^2	S	Vnf
/lōhkinki	gaḍḍi	kōysi,/
for houses	grass	having cut

CLVf:

	O^2			S	O^2	Vf
/ā	peldiki	ittagudēta	payya	gangāl	endanānki	vattōṇḍu./
that	marriage for	of village	name	personal name	for dancing	he came

CLVnf:

Tw	O^2	Vnf
/aske	ḍōlīn	vēnsōmatku,/
then	drums	while playing

CLVnf:

O^1	O^2	Vnf
/pēnkinki	dālguḍḍān	singirisi,/
for gods	red god cloths	having decorated

CLVf:

O^2	O^2	Vf
/kōrkini	paddīni	tēyitōru./
cocks	pigs	they will bring

CLVf:

Po	Po	Vf
/gaḍḍētagga	lingukiniporro	vaḍipitōṇḍu./
platform near	lingus on	he will wipe off

CLVnf:

S	Vnf
/nanna	puṭṭovāke,/
I	not having been born

CLVf:

Tw	O^1	O^1	S	Vf
/agga	dāyanānki	nāku	isṭam	ille./
there	for going	to me	liking	is not

CLVf:

S		O^2		Ab	Vf
/mā	talli	māminni	ī	rōgātkunci	viḍipisa./
our	mother	us	this	disease from	release

CLVnf:

O^2	O^2	Vnf
/gūṇḍru	gūṇḍru	injōre,/
grunt	grunt	saying

5.5. The phrase (PH). In addition to clauses, a sentence may contain the following phrase constructions: connective phrases, interjectory phrases, response phrases, and noun phrases.

1. Connective phrases (ConPH). Connective phrases are comprised of any connective (Con) followed by /,/. Connective phrases are always bound, and occur before other elements of the sentence.

Examples: /<u>ganaka</u>, tungoḍḍu/ '<u>therefore</u>, don't do'
/<u>goni</u>, varrōṇḍu/ '<u>but</u>, he won't come'

2. Interjectory phrases (InPH). Interjectory phrases consist of any interjection (In) followed by /./. The interjectory phrase is free and equivalent to a minor sentence type.

Examples: /ayyo./ 'alas!'
/sare./ 'OK'

3. Response phrases (RPH). Response phrases consist of any S, O, L, Sc, Ab or Adv followed by /./ and preceded by silence. The response phrase is free and coterminous with a minor sentence type. Semantically, it is a response to a previous utterance.

Examples: /inje./ 'now'
/nanna./ 'I'
/lōte./ 'in house'
/miminni./ 'you'

4. Noun phrases (NPH). Noun phrases consist of any N, PN, or Nn followed by another N, PN, or Nn with which it agrees in person, number and gender. Preceding either of these N, PN or Nn's may be any acceptable sequence of S, O, Ab, L or Tw. The NPH occurs either in immediate constituency with another NPH, CL, or /./. The NPH may thus be coordinate with a major sentence type. Although the NPH is structurally equivalent to a CLVf, where V is the verb mann 'to be', its semantic range is not equivalent. Whereas a CLVf with mann asserts the existence of some prior noun or pronoun, the NPH asserts an equivalence or identity relation between the first and second N, PN, or Nn. Formally, this is similar to the difference between the statement: "There is an x, and x exists", and the statement: "there is an x and there is a y such that x is equivalent to y". It should be noted that this relation is consistent in the negative. Negation of mann 'to be', is accomplished by its suppletive form ill 'to be not', but, an NPH is negated by the negative tense-mode of ā 'to become'. The personal ending suffix of ā in this case is congruent in person, number, and gender with the NPH.

Example: NPH:

PN Adj PN
/ōṇḍu cinna ōṇḍu./
he small he, i.e., 'he is small', 'he is a small one'

PN N
/iddu bātādi./ (i.e., a "nominalized" adverb. Adv + PE, 3.79)
it what it, i.e., 'what is this'

PN N
/iddu orroṭi./ (i.e., a "nominalized" numeral, 3.54)
it one it, i.e., 'this is the only one'

PN	N	
/iddu	mencidi./	(i.e., a "nominalized" adjective, 3.79)
it	good it,	i.e., 'this is good'

PN	N
/ivvu	mencivi./
they	good they, i.e., 'these are good'

	Nn		Nn
/ī	guḍḍa	erra	guḍḍa./
this	cloth	red	cloth, i.e., 'this cloth is a red cloth'

	Nn	N
/ī	guḍḍa	erraṭi./
this	cloth	red it, i.e., 'this cloth is a red one'

PN	N
/iddu	nādi/
this	my it, i.e., 'this is mine'

PN	N
/ivvu	nāvi/
this	my these, i.e., 'these are mine'

PN	Nn
/ōṇḍu	vādanōṇḍu/
he	comes he, i.e., 'he is the one who comes'

N	N
/ēlāḍi	talaptaddu/
younger sister	asked it, i.e., 'younger sister is the one who asked'

Tw	S	O^1	S
/ninne	ōṇḍu	iggeṭiki	attōṇḍu/
yesterday	he	to here	came he, i.e., 'he is the one who came here yesterday'

When the initial N in an NPH is a pronoun, there are special forms of the feminine/neuter, first person singular and plural, and second person singular and plural when these are preceded by a verbal adjective.

Examples:

/nanna tunganōninni/	'I am the one (male) who does'
/nanna tungānidāninni/	'I am the one (female) who does'
/mīru tunganōru/	'you (pl.) are the one who does'
/mamma tunganōramu/	'we are the ones who do'
/nimma tunganōninni/	'you (sg.) male are the one who does'
/nimma tungānidāninni/	'you (sg.) female are the one who does'

These are all cases of agreement between the two noun constituents, but the interesting aspect is the fact that most of these involve some form of the accusative pronoun. This would possibly imply that rather than an identity of subjects, what is involved is an identity between subject and object.

There are other cases of apparent lack of agreement between the noun constituents of an NPH.

Examples:

/ōṇḍu kettādi/	'that he said', 'the fact of his saying'
/nanna attādi/	'that I went', 'the fact of my going'
/mīru vattādi/	'that you came', 'the fact of your coming'

If these were to conform to the equivalence between congruent nouns, we would expect respectively:

/ōṇḍu kettōṇḍu/
/nanna attōninni/
/miru attōru/

The solution here is simply that the first three items do not represent noun phrases. The forms kettādi, attādi, vattādi are verbal adjectives plus the pronominal suffix //TI// (3.54).

5.6. The sentence (SEN). Sentences have /./ as one immediate constituent. Other immediate constituents are given with sentence types below. There are two sentence types: major and minor.

Minor sentences. Minor sentences do not contain a Vf. They consist of interjectory phrases and response phrases which are semantically bound to a preceding utterance.

Examples: SEN. InPH
/ayyo./ 'alas!'

RPH
/inje./ 'now'

RPH
/mādi./ 'mine'

Major sentences. Major sentences have two subtypes. The first subtype contains a Vf.

Examples: SEN. CLVf
/rāsitāna/ 'I will write'
/ōṇḍu igge vattōṇḍu/ 'he came here'

ConPH CLVf
/ganaka, rāsoddu./ 'therefore, don't write'
/gōni, kettōṇḍu./ 'but, he told'

SEN: NPH CLVf
/ōṇḍu mā lōtki vādanōṇḍu, inje varrōṇḍu./
'he used to come to my house, now he won't come'

CLVnf CLVf
/nanna lōtki anji, vāyitāna./
'having gone to (my) house, I will come'

CLAdv CLVf
/kallu otta payya, andōru uttōru/
'after bringing palm wine everyone drank'

The second major sentence subtype does not contain a Vf. Instead, it consists of an NPH in immediate constituency with /./.

Examples: SEN: NPH
/nanna rāsanōninni./
'I am the one who (used to write) writes'

ConPH NPH
/gōni, ōṇḍu tunganōṇḍu./
'but he is the one who (used to do) does'

CLVnf NPH
/ālā tungtkanna, ōru vīyavasāyam tunganōru/
'although they are doing like that (now), they used to do cultivation'

CLAdv NPH
/dōḍa tittapayya, ōru kallu uṇdanōru/
'after eating cooked rice, they are the ones who (used to) drink palm wine'

Complex major sentences consist of more than one CLVnf, CLAdv, or NPH preceding the CLVf or NPH. Presumably, the number of CLVnf or CLAdv preceding a CLVf or NPH is unlimited, though the maximum recorded in texts is twenty-two. Sentences containing more than one NPH are rare, but sentences containing more than one CLVnf or CLAdv before an NPH are quite frequent. The occurrence of preceding clauses and noun phrases is free. Since the order of occurrence is not restricted, sentences containing more than one clause are formally equivalent to simple sentences.

Examples: SEN: CLVnf CLVnf CLVnf CLVf
/ōṇḍu vāsi, pani tungi, uḍḍi, attōṇḍu./
'he having come, having done work, having turned about, he went'

SEN: CLAdv CLVnf CLVf

/mirtapayya, māmāni lōtki vāsi, agge kāpuram tungtōṇḍu./

'after running (away), having come to mother's brother's house, there residence he did'

CLAdv CLVnf NPH

/mallu tēdtagga, ūḍtku, ōṇḍu aggeṭiki vādanōṇḍu./

'peacock where had flown if saw he to there he used to go'

APPENDIX A

TEXT ANALYSIS

The following text fragment is analyzed in terms of constructions and grammatical units. References to the grammar are indicated by the appropriate section number. No reference is made to morphophonemic process or to phonemicization. Utterances within // // are written morphophonemically with upper case letters as cover symbols for alternating morphemes. Utterances within ( ) contain the appropriate morpheme alternate. Utterances within / / are phonemic realizations of morphophonemic processes denoted by morphophonemic process cover symbols occurring within // // and ( ). The phonetic level marked by [ ] is omitted.

1. iddu pēnu paṇḍum tungāni tīru.

2. pēnu vaḍḍe gōtra beriyatōru pēnu paṇḍum tunganānki orro nēṇḍu andōru kudi, ōdisitōru.

3. bēdōrro rōju paṇḍum tunganānki erparsitōru.

4. ā nēṇḍu ḍōlīrini pāṭēdīni karringisi, pēnu mandētagganji, pēnu vaḍḍe jallaka vaḍḍe iruvūru ginna ā sēkatōrantā pēnu mandēsi, aluku vāṭi, gaḍḍe tohci, ūsi, pēnu gaḍḍāni porrotnunci dippi, gobbe tōmi, jalli tohci, dālguḍḍān tohci, ḍōlīru ḍōlīn vēnsōmatku, pāṭēdi kinnēri gissōmatku, guggilam pōga vāṭōmatku, pēnkinki dālguḍḍān singirisi, gaḍḍētporro vāṭi, aḍivīte gubbāltporro mannāni lingukini tattanānki pēnu vaḍḍe jallaka vaḍḍe ḍōlīru inka beriyatōru ḍōlīn vēnsōre anji, lingukini baṇḍa serrēt nunci bāydiki tīsi, pālde nūrsi, pasupu rāsi, kōḍīni kōysi, netturu vāṇṭpōrro tōsi, guggilam pōga vāṭi lingukini kotta gontāte gibbi, kotta guḍḍāte bābu tohtitōru.

Free Translation:

1. This is the method of doing the god festival.

2. The lineage priest and elders will sit down and decide on a day for doing the god festival.

3. They will arrange one day or another for doing the festival.

4. (On) that day they will call the drummer people and the lineage bard, go to the god shed (where) both the lineage priest and lineage mother's brother as well as all male members of the lineage branch sweep the god shed, smear (it) with cow dung, build a platform, smear (it), take the god bells down from above, clean the small pot, tie (on) yak tail and red cloths, and while the drummers drum and bards saw (on their) violins, and guggilam (resin of the shorea robusta) smoke is coming, they decorate the gods, put them on the platform, and to bring the gods which were being kept on a hillock in the forest, the lineage priest and lineage mother's brother, the drummers, also elders go while the drums are playing, take the gods out of the rock crevices, bathe (them) in milk, mark (them with) tumeric, sacrifice fowls, pour their blood on them (the gods), bathe (them) in guggilam smoke, stuff the gods into a new (bamboo) tube and tie them across their bodies with a new piece of cloth.

1.

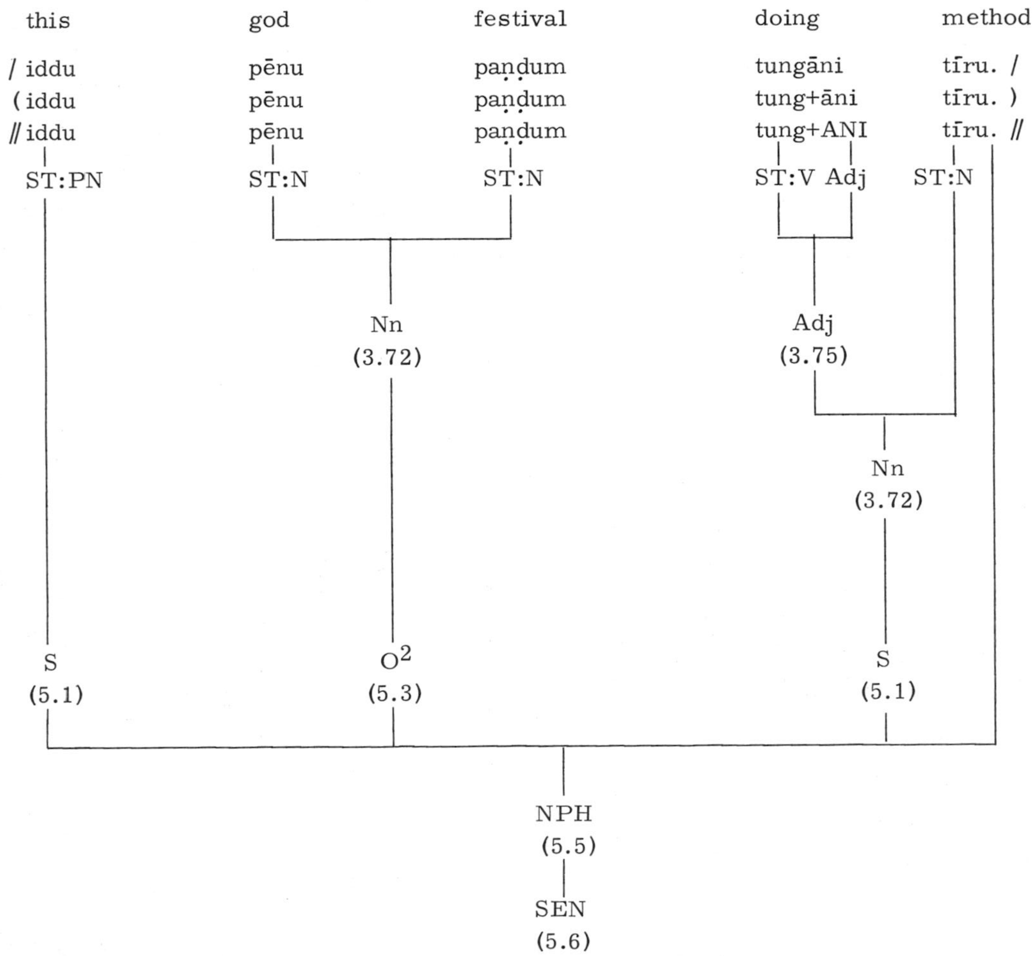
this
god
festival
doing
method
/ iddu
pēnu
paṇḍum
tungāni
tīru. /
(iddu
pēnu
paṇḍum
tung+āni
tīru.)
// iddu
pēnu
paṇḍum
tung+ANI
tīru. //
ST:PN
ST:N
ST:N
ST:V Adj
ST:N
Nn
(3.72)
Adj
(3.75)
Nn
(3.72)
S
(5.1)
O2
(5.3)
S
(5.1)
NPH
(5.5)
SEN
(5.6)

2. god priest lineage elders god festival for doing one day all having sat, they will decide.

/pēnu vaḍḍe gōtra beriyatōru pēnu panḍum tunganānki orro nēnḍu andōru kudi , ōdisitōru./
(pēnu vaḍḍe gōtra beriya+t+ōru pēnu panḍum tung+anā+n+ki orro nēnḍu andōru kud+i , ōdisitōru.)
//pēnu vaḍḍe gōtra beriya+T+ōru pēnu panḍum tung + AN + IN+KI orro nēnḍu andōru kud+CI , ōdis IT ORU//

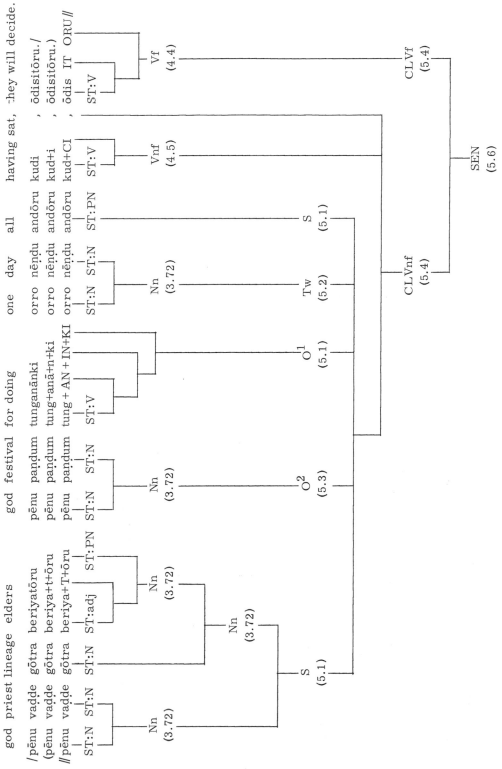

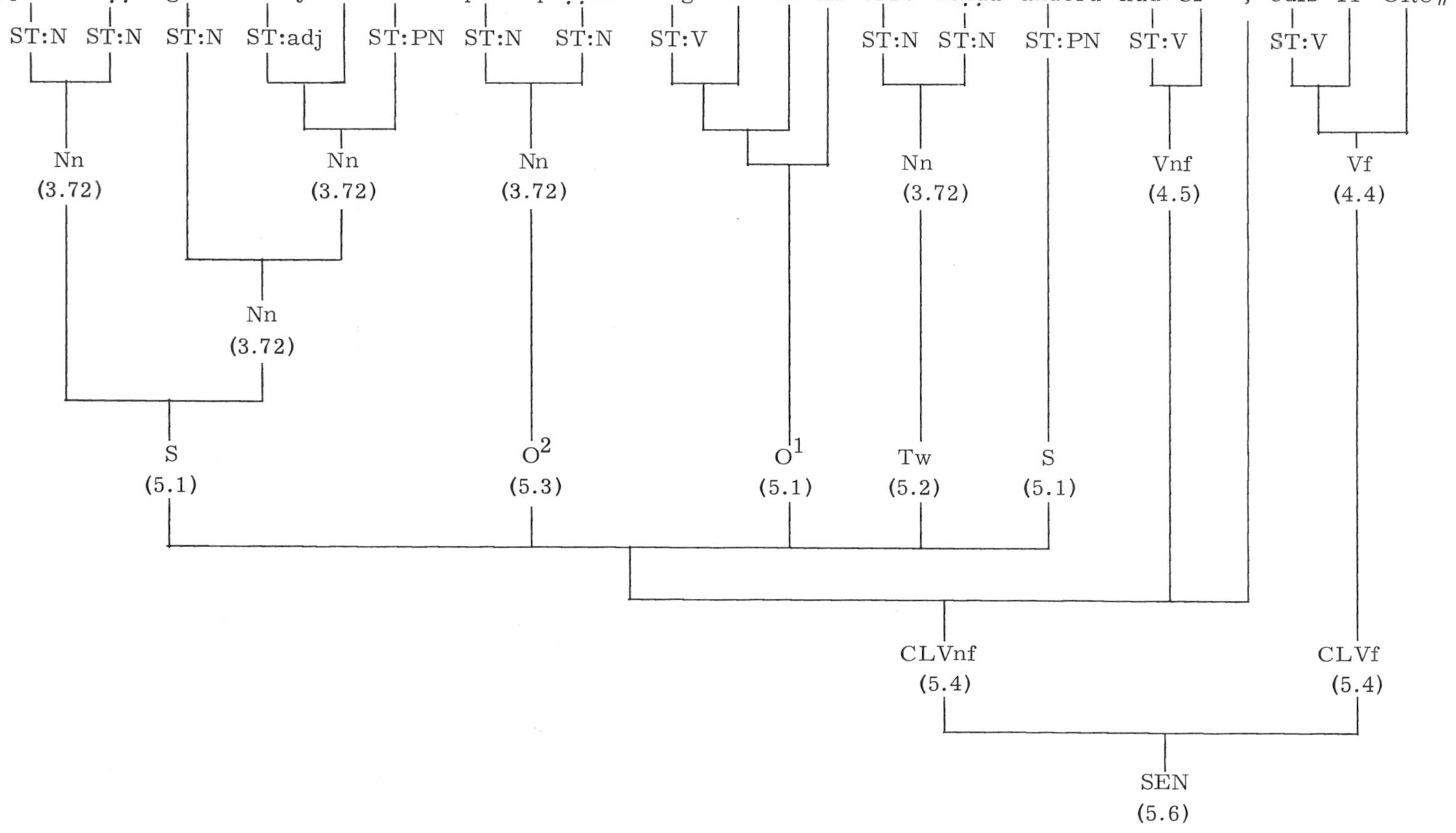

3. some one day festival for doing they will arrange

/bēdōrro   rōju   paṇḍum   tunganānki   erparsitōru./
(bēdō`orro   rōju   paṇḍum   tung+anā+n+ki   erpars+it+ōru.)
// bēdu + ō`orro   rōju   paṇḍum   tung + AN + IN+KI   erpars+IT+ORU. //

ST:PN   Cl   ST:N   ST:N   ST:N   ST:V   ST:V

PN   Nn
(3.56)   (3.72)

O² O² O² O¹   Vf
(5.3) (5.3) (5.3) (5.1)   (4.4)

CLVf
(5.4)

SEN
(5.6)

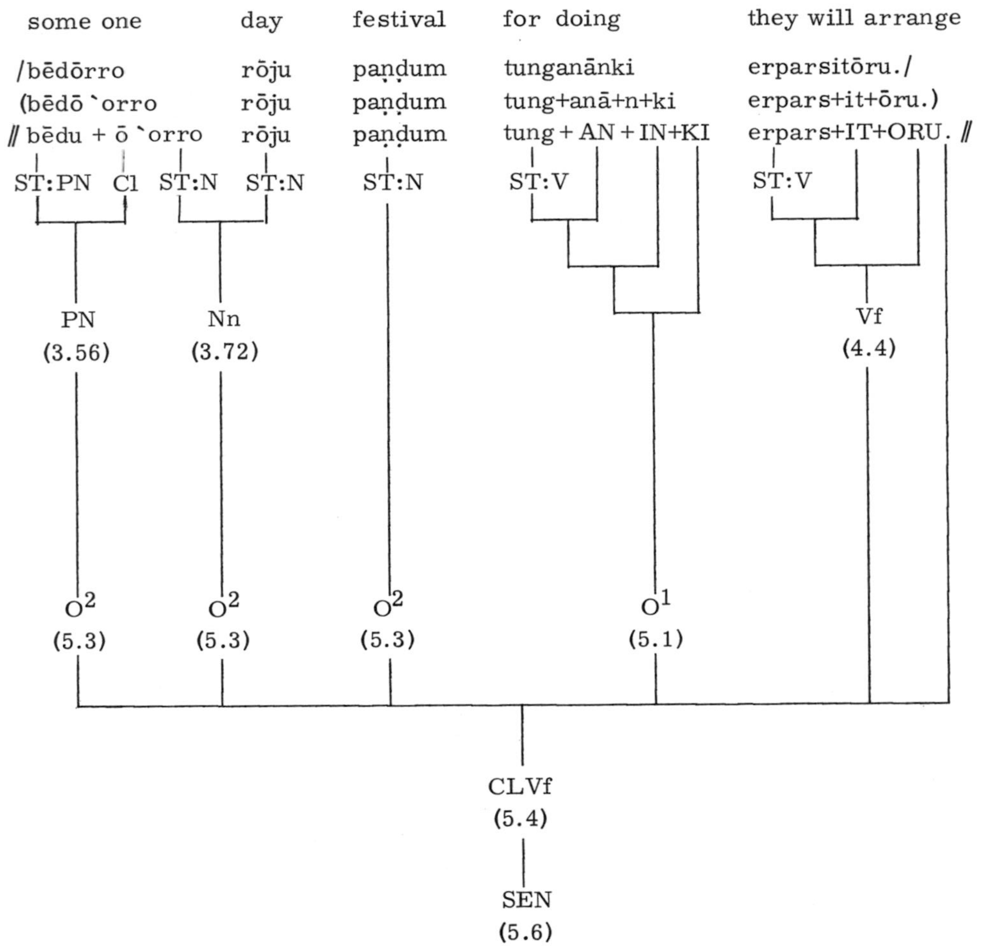

4. that day drummers bard having called, god shed near having gone,

/ ā nēndu ḍōlīrini pāṭēdīni karringisi , pēnu mandētagganji , /
(ā nēndu ḍōli`+īru´+in+i pāṭēdī+n+i karringis+i , pēnu mandē+t+agga` anji ,)
// ā nēndu ḍōli`+ORU´+IN+NI pāṭēdi+IN+NI karringis+CI , pēnu mande+T+agga` dā+CI , //

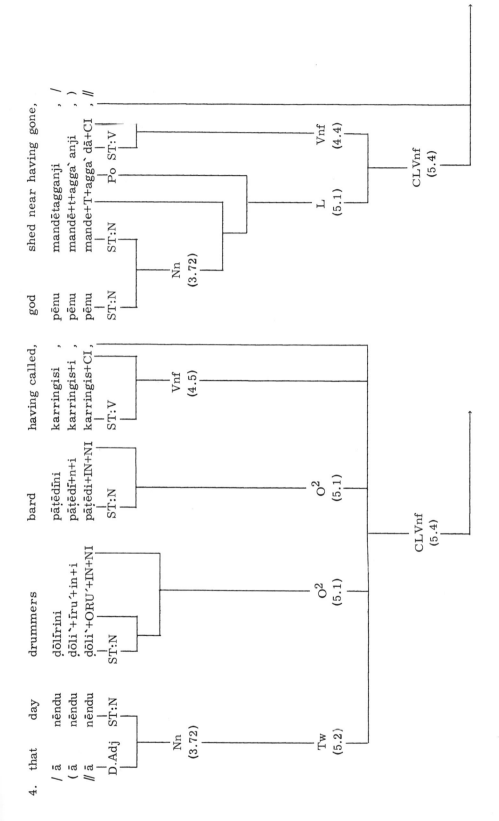

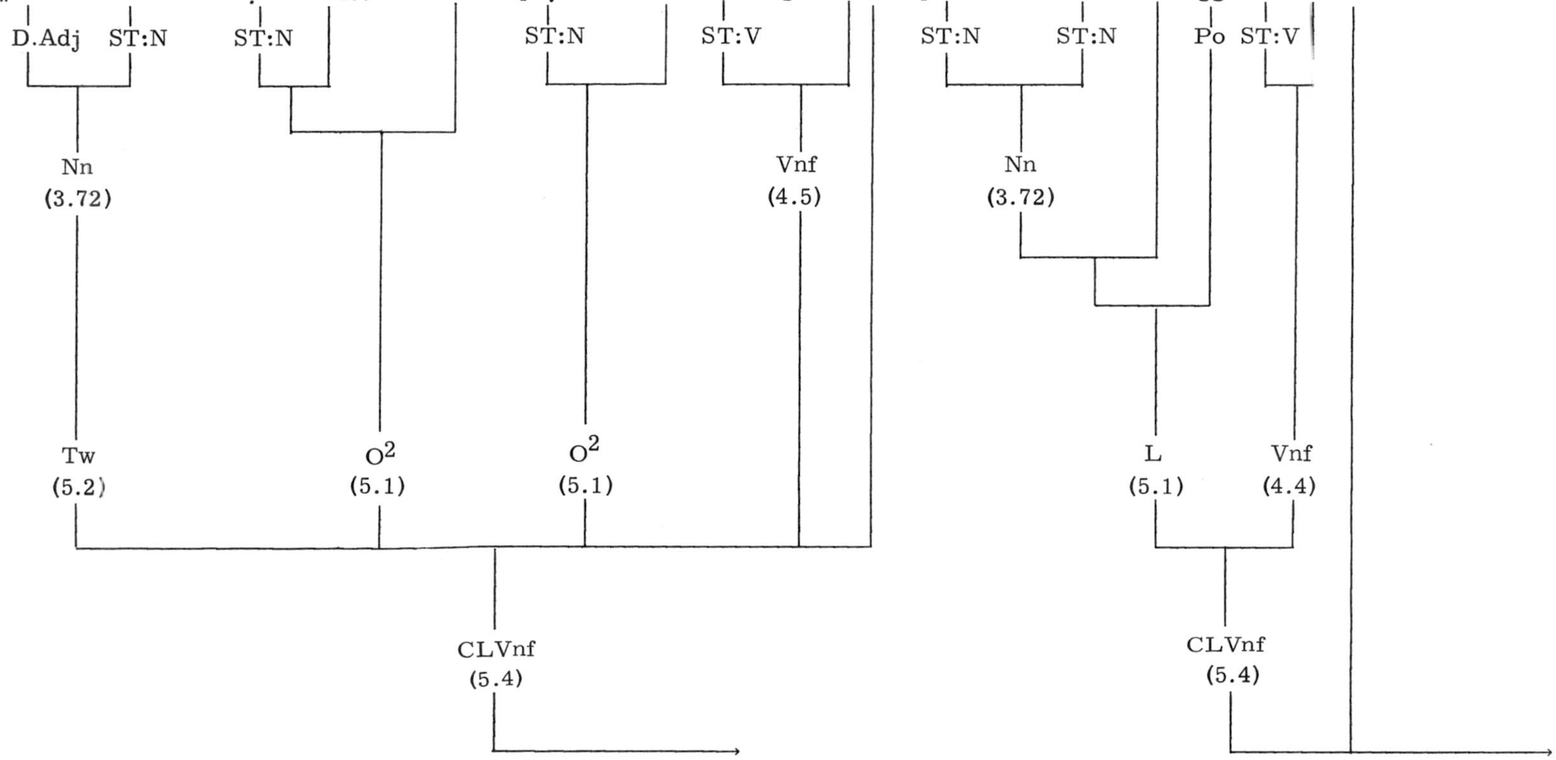

4. (continued)

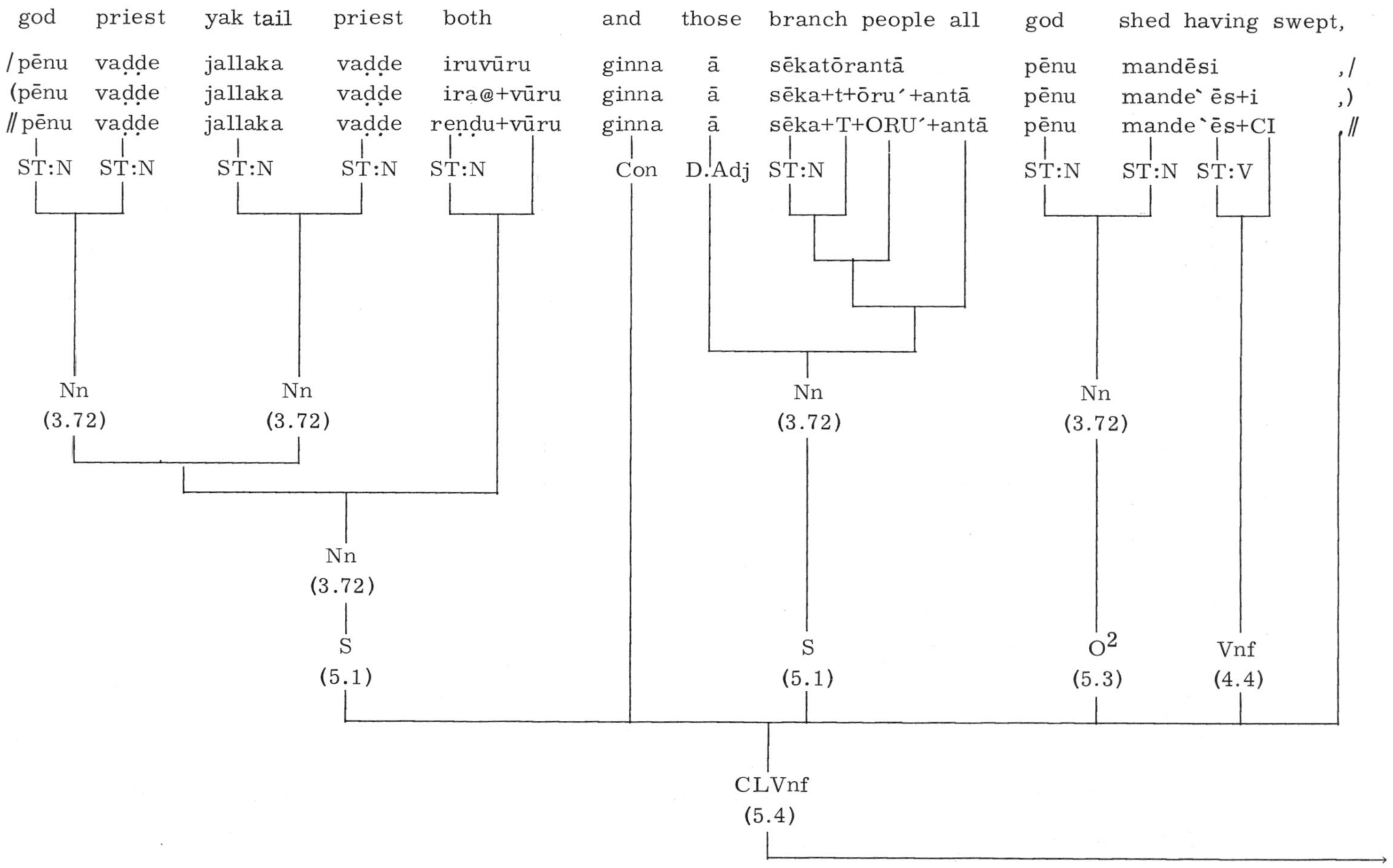
god priest yak tail priest both and those branch people all god shed having swept,
/pēnu vaḍḍe jallaka vaḍḍe iruvūru ginna ā sēkatōrantā pēnu mandēsi ,/
(pēnu vaḍḍe jallaka vaḍḍe ira@+vūru ginna ā sēka+t+ōru´+antā pēnu mande` ēs+i ,)
//pēnu vaḍḍe jallaka vaḍḍe reṇḍu+vūru ginna ā sēka+T+ORU´+antā pēnu mande`ēs+CI ,//
ST:N ST:N ST:N ST:N ST:N Con D.Adj ST:N ST:N ST:N ST:V
Nn (3.72)
Nn (3.72)
Nn (3.72)
Nn (3.72)
Nn (3.72)
S (5.1)
S (5.1)
O2 (5.3)
Vnf (4.4)
CLVnf (5.4)

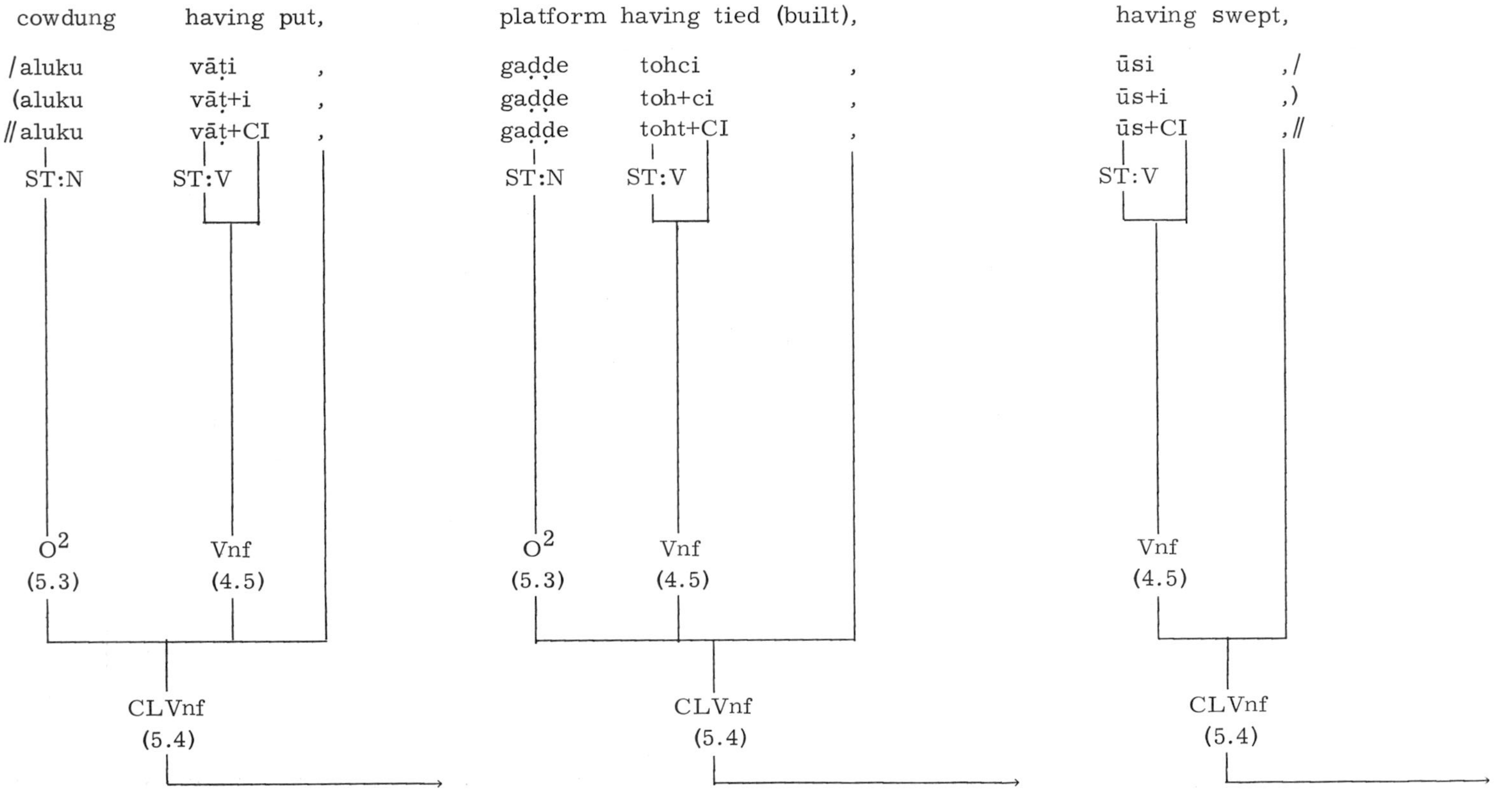
cowdung having put,
platform having tied (built),
having swept,
/aluku vāṭi ,
(aluku vāṭ+i ,
//aluku vāṭ+CI ,
gaḍḍe tohci ,
gaḍḍe toh+ci ,
gaḍḍe toht+CI ,
ūsi ,/
ūs+i ,)
ūs+CI ,//
ST:N
ST:V
ST:N
ST:V
ST:V
O2
(5.3)
Vnf
(4.5)
O2
(5.3)
Vnf
(4.5)
Vnf
(4.5)
CLVnf
(5.4)
CLVnf
(5.4)
CLVnf
(5.4)

4. (continued)

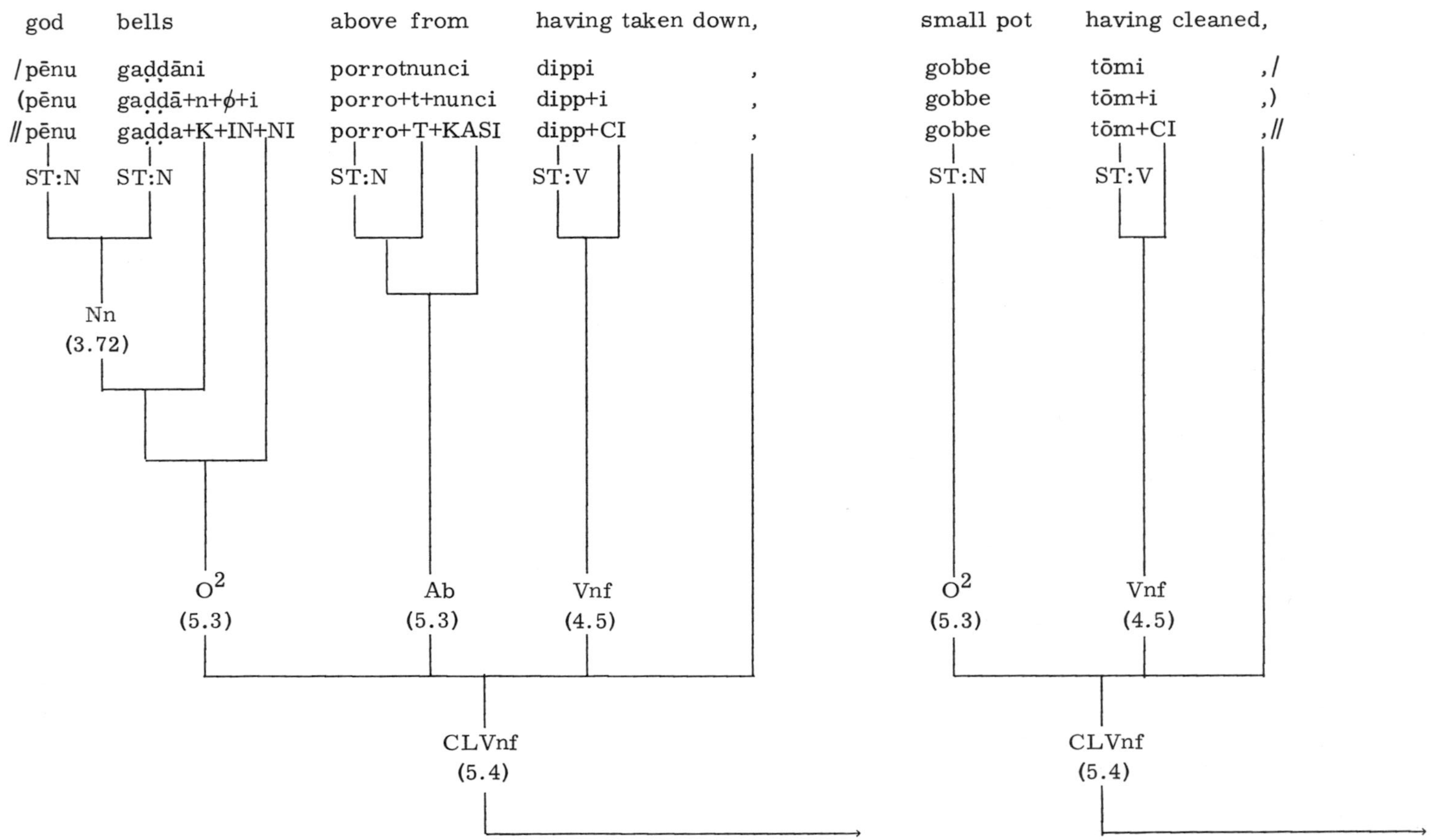
god bells above from having taken down, small pot having cleaned,
/pēnu gaḍḍāni porrotnunci dippi , gobbe tōmi ,/
(pēnu gaḍḍā+n+ϕ+i porro+t+nunci dipp+i , gobbe tōm+i ,)
//pēnu gaḍḍa+K+IN+NI porro+T+KASI dipp+CI , gobbe tōm+CI ,//
ST:N ST:N ST:N ST:V ST:N ST:V
Nn (3.72)
O2 (5.3) Ab (5.3) Vnf (4.5) O2 (5.3) Vnf (4.5)
CLVnf (5.4) CLVnf (5.4)

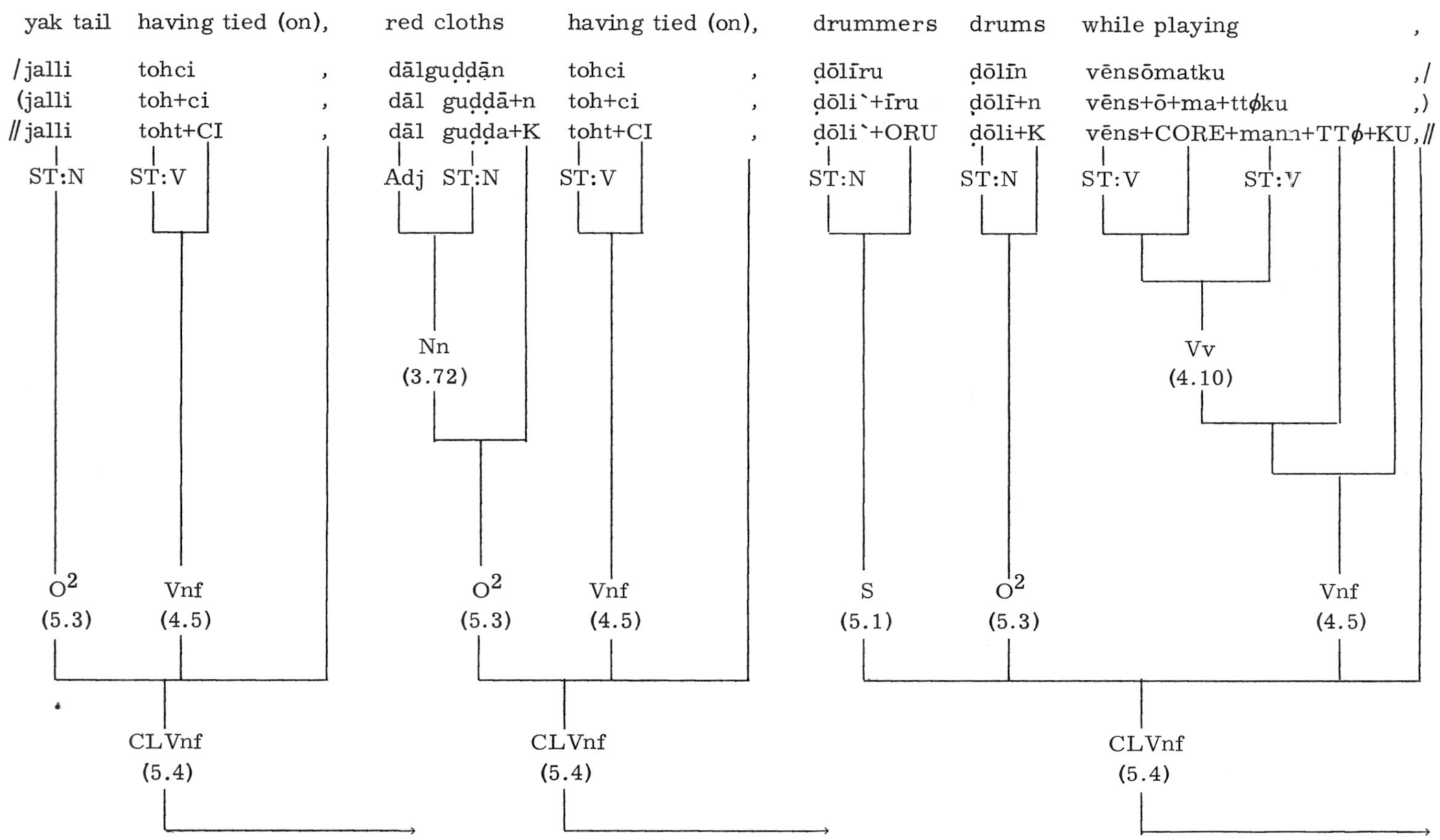

yak tail having tied (on), red cloths having tied (on), drummers drums while playing ,
/jalli tohci , dālguḍḍān tohci , ḍōlīru ḍōlīn vēnsōmatku ,/
(jalli toh+ci , dāl guḍḍā+n toh+ci , ḍōli`+īru ḍōlī+n vēns+ō+ma+ttϕku ,)
//jalli toht+CI , dāl guḍḍa+K toht+CI , ḍōli`+ORU ḍōli+K vēns+CORE+mann+TTϕ+KU,//
ST:N
ST:V
Adj
ST:N
ST:V
ST:N
ST:N
ST:V
ST:V
Nn
(3.72)
Vv
(4.10)
O2
(5.3)
Vnf
(4.5)
O2
(5.3)
Vnf
(4.5)
S
(5.1)
O2
(5.3)
Vnf
(4.5)
CLVnf
(5.4)
CLVnf
(5.4)
CLVnf
(5.4)

4. (continued)

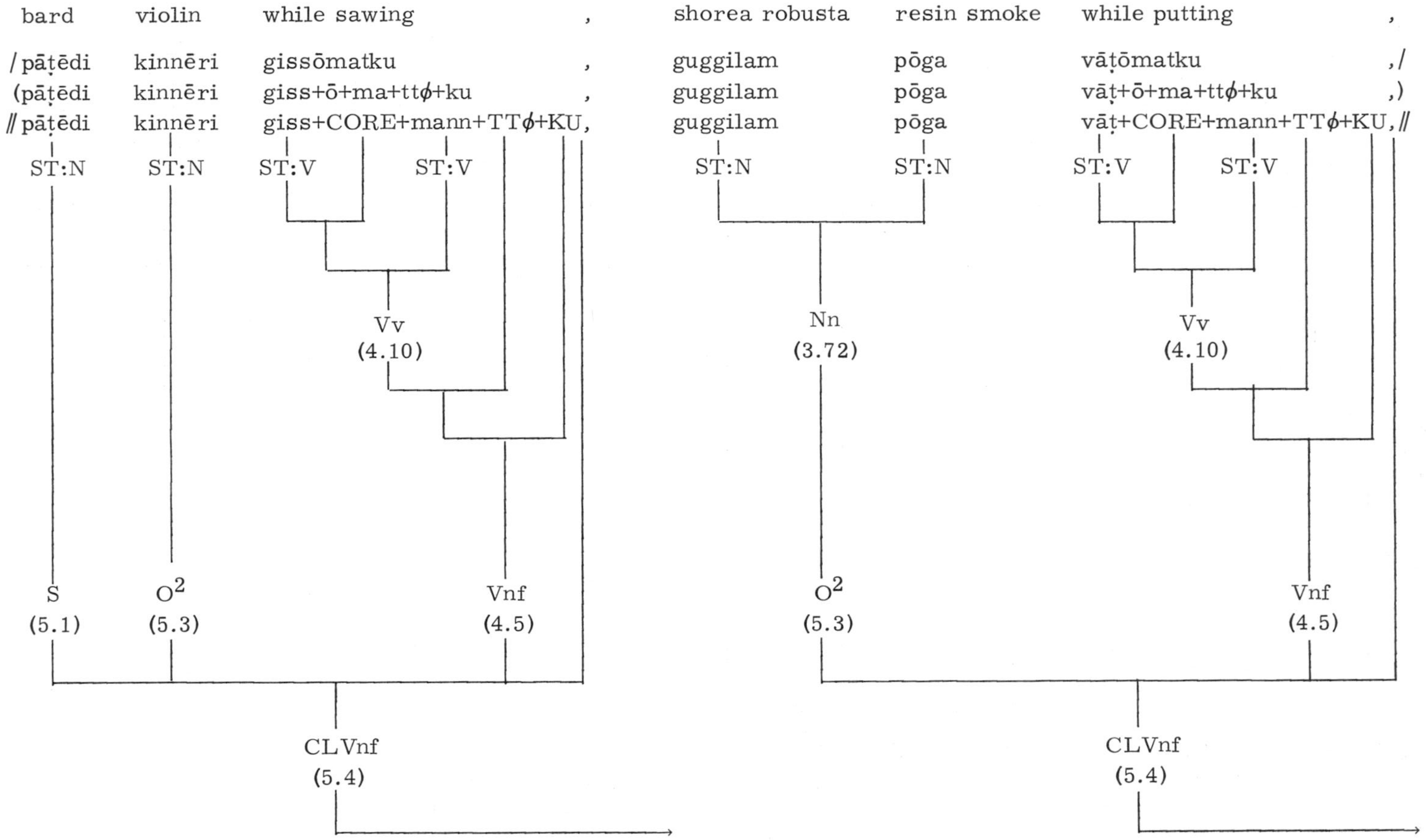
bard violin while sawing ,
/pāṭēdi kinnēri gissōmatku ,
(pāṭēdi kinnēri giss+ō+ma+ttϕ+ku ,
//pāṭēdi kinnēri giss+CORE+mann+TTϕ+KU,
ST:N ST:N ST:V ST:V
Vv (4.10)
S (5.1) O2 (5.3) Vnf (4.5)
CLVnf (5.4)
shorea robusta resin smoke while putting ,
guggilam pōga vāṭōmatku ,/
guggilam pōga vāṭ+ō+ma+ttϕ+ku ,)
guggilam pōga vāṭ+CORE+mann+TTϕ+KU,//
ST:N ST:N ST:V ST:V
Nn (3.72)
Vv (4.10)
O2 (5.3) Vnf (4.5)
CLVnf (5.4)

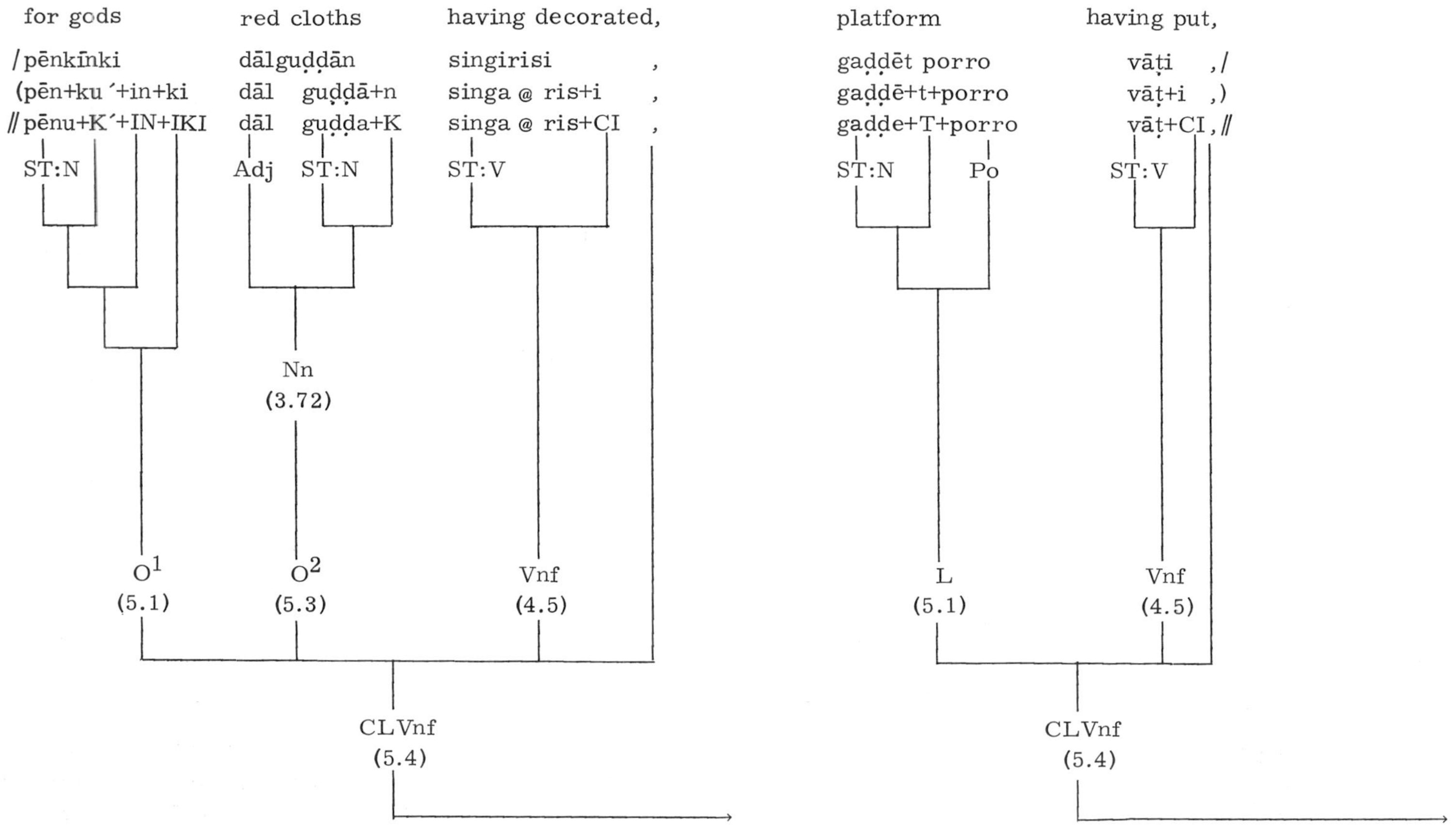

for gods
/pēnkīnki
(pēn+ku´+in+ki
//pēnu+K´+IN+IKI
ST:N
red cloths
dālguḍḍān
dāl guḍḍā+n
dāl guḍḍa+K
Adj
ST:N
Nn
(3.72)
having decorated,
singirisi ,
singa @ ris+i ,
singa @ ris+CI ,
ST:V
O1
(5.1)
O2
(5.3)
Vnf
(4.5)
CLVnf
(5.4)
platform
gaḍḍēt porro
gaḍḍē+t+porro
gaḍḍe+T+porro
ST:N
Po
having put,
vāṭi ,/
vāṭ+i ,)
vāṭ+CI ,//
ST:V
L
(5.1)
Vnf
(4.5)
CLVnf
(5.4)

4. (continued)

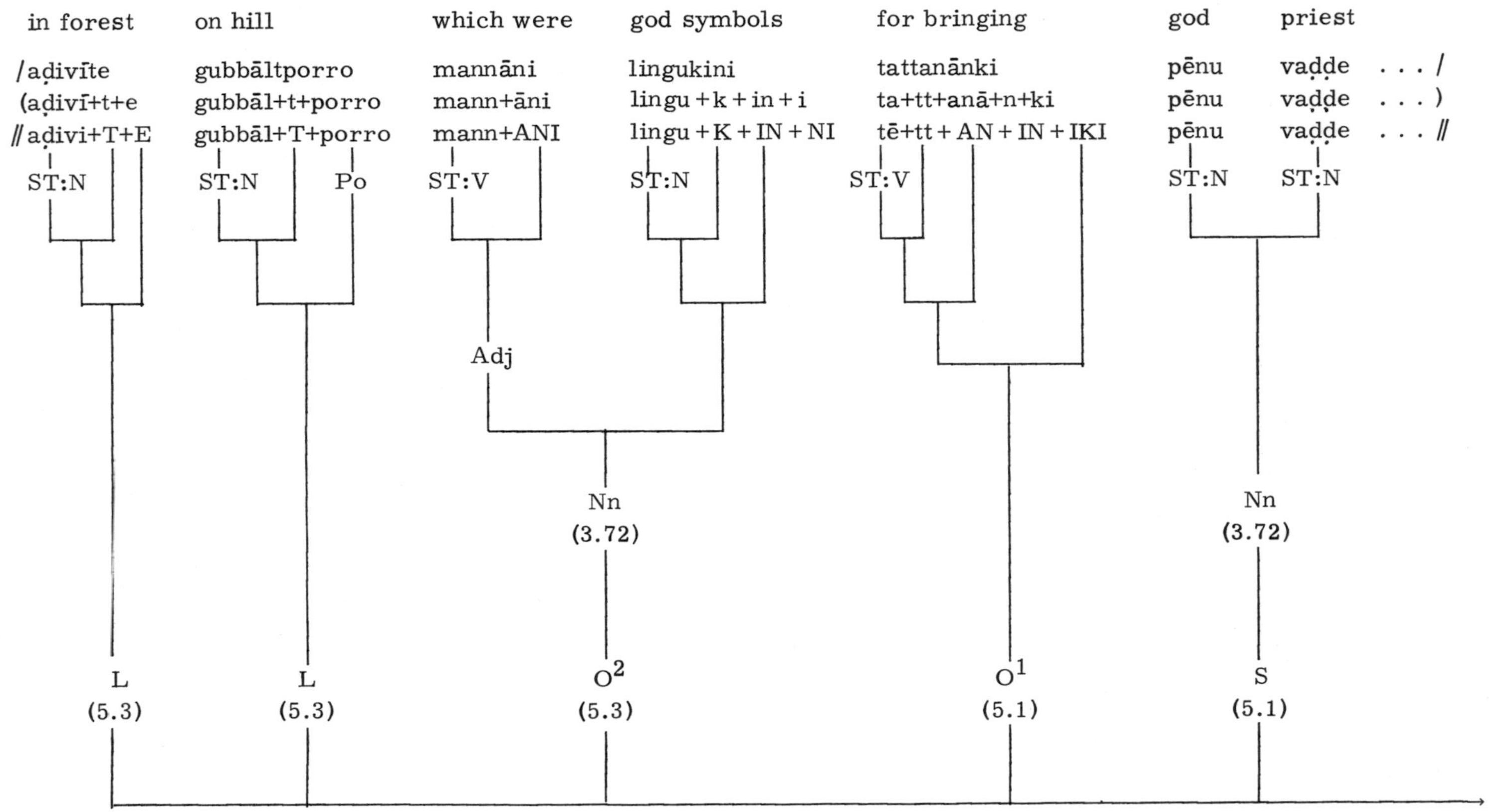
in forest
/aḍivīte
(aḍivī+t+e
//aḍivi+T+E
ST:N
on hill
gubbāltporro
gubbāl+t+porro
gubbāl+T+porro
ST:N
Po
which were
mannāni
mann+āni
mann+ANI
ST:V
Adj
god symbols
lingukini
lingu + k + in + i
lingu + K + IN + NI
ST:N
for bringing
tattanānki
ta+tt+anā+n+ki
tē+tt + AN + IN + IKI
ST:V
god
pēnu
pēnu
pēnu
ST:N
priest
vaḍḍe . . . /
vaḍḍe . . .)
vaḍḍe . . . //
ST:N
Nn
(3.72)
Nn
(3.72)
L
(5.3)
L
(5.3)
O2
(5.3)
O1
(5.1)
S
(5.1)

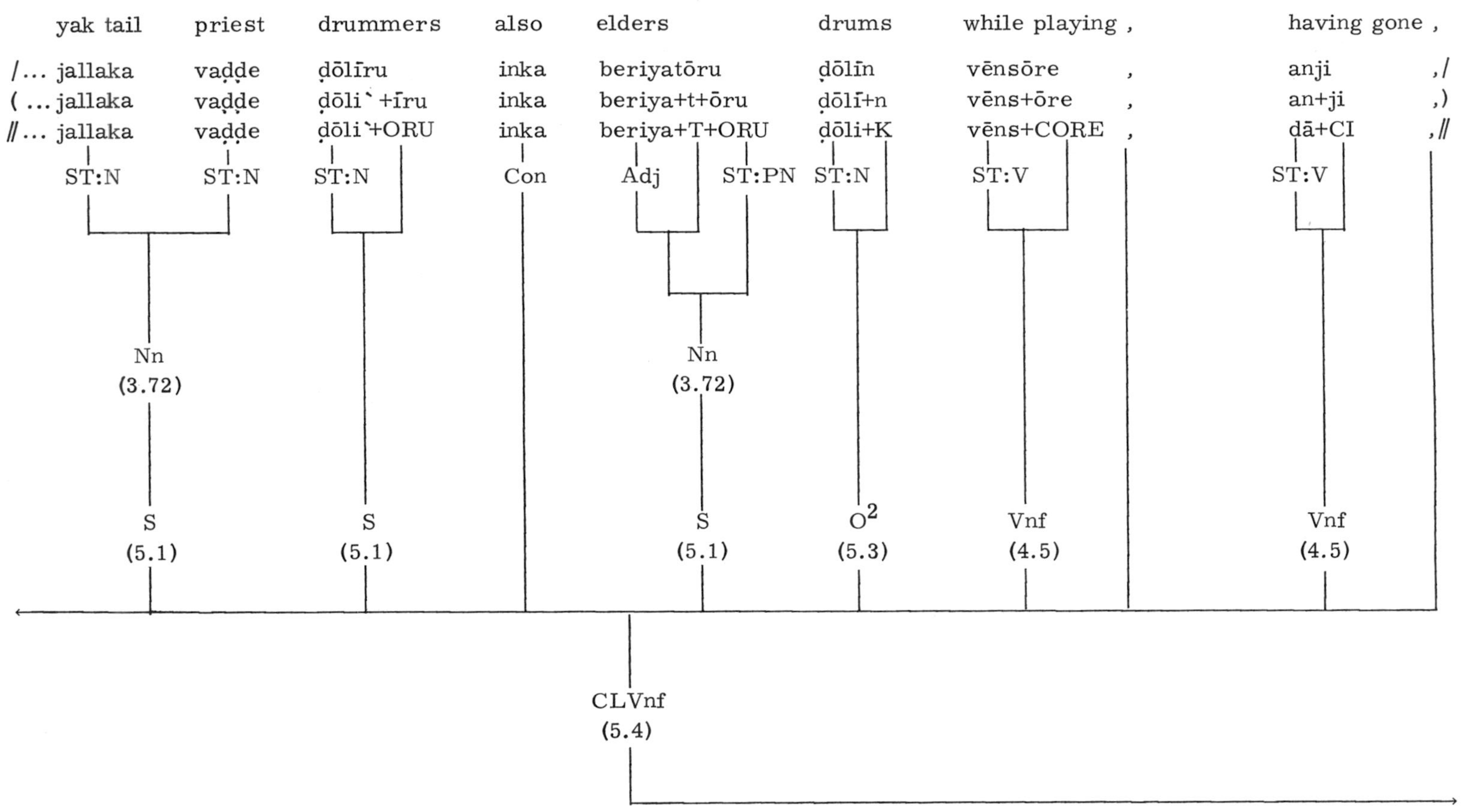

yak tail
priest
drummers
also
elders
drums
while playing ,
having gone ,
/... jallaka
vaḍḍe
ḍōlīru
inka
beriyatōru
ḍōlīn
vēnsōre ,
anji ,/
(... jallaka
vaḍḍe
ḍōli` +īru
inka
beriya+t+ōru
ḍōlī+n
vēns+ōre ,
an+ji ,)
//... jallaka
vaḍḍe
ḍōli`+ORU
inka
beriya+T+ORU
ḍōli+K
vēns+CORE ,
dā+CI ,//
ST:N
ST:N
ST:N
Con
Adj
ST:PN
ST:N
ST:V
ST:V
Nn
(3.72)
Nn
(3.72)
S
(5.1)
S
(5.1)
S
(5.1)
O2
(5.3)
Vnf
(4.5)
Vnf
(4.5)
CLVnf
(5.4)

4. (continued)

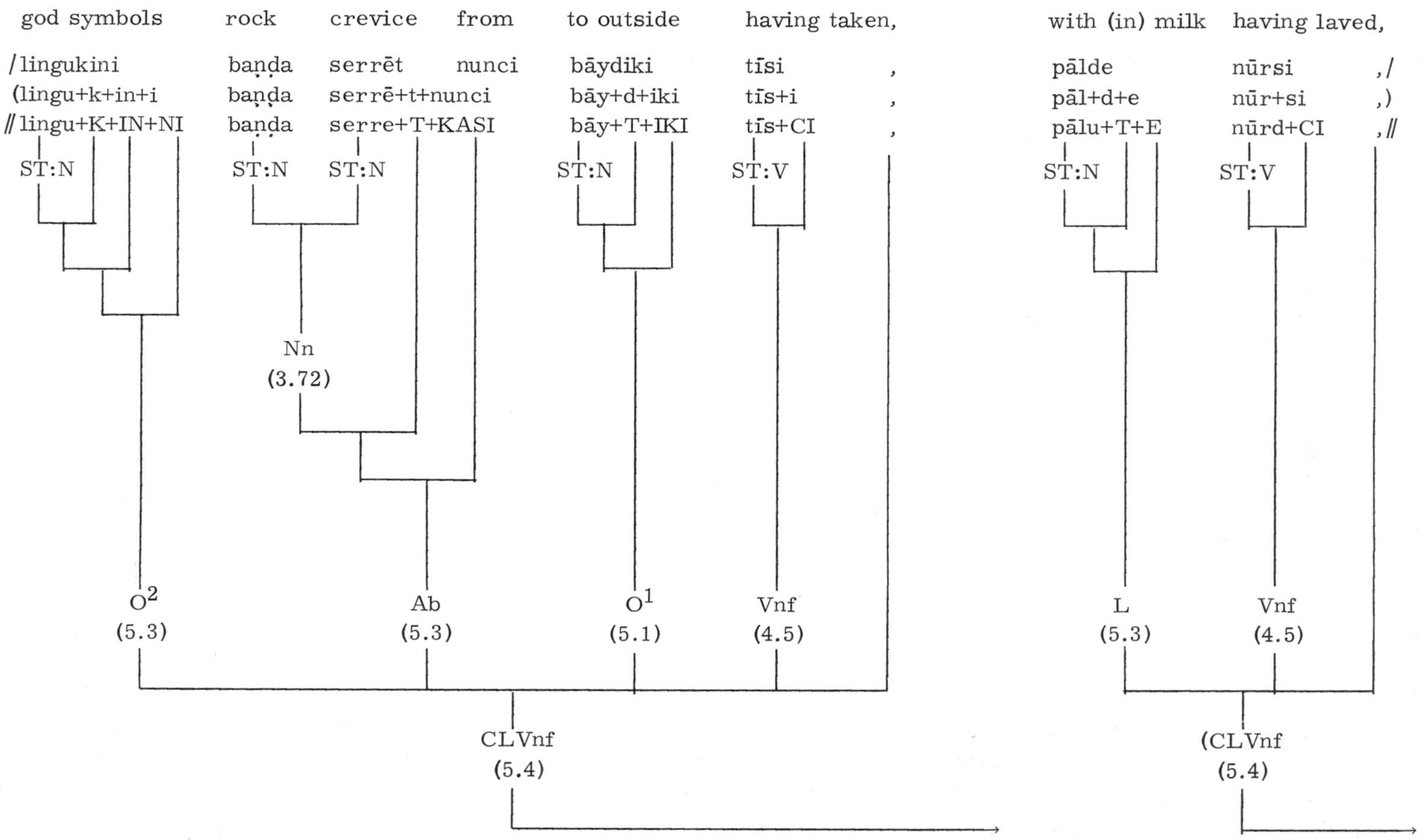
god symbols
rock
crevice
from
to outside
having taken,
with (in) milk
having laved,
/lingukini
(lingu+k+in+i
//lingu+K+IN+NI
banḍa
banḍa
banḍa
serrēt
serrē+t+nunci
serre+T+KASI
nunci
bāydiki
bāy+d+iki
bāy+T+IKI
tīsi
tīs+i
tīs+CI
pālde
pāl+d+e
pālu+T+E
nūrsi ,/
nūr+si ,)
nūrd+CI ,//
ST:N
ST:V
Nn
(3.72)
O2
(5.3)
Ab
(5.3)
O1
(5.1)
Vnf
(4.5)
L
(5.3)
Vnf
(4.5)
CLVnf
(5.4)
(CLVnf
(5.4)

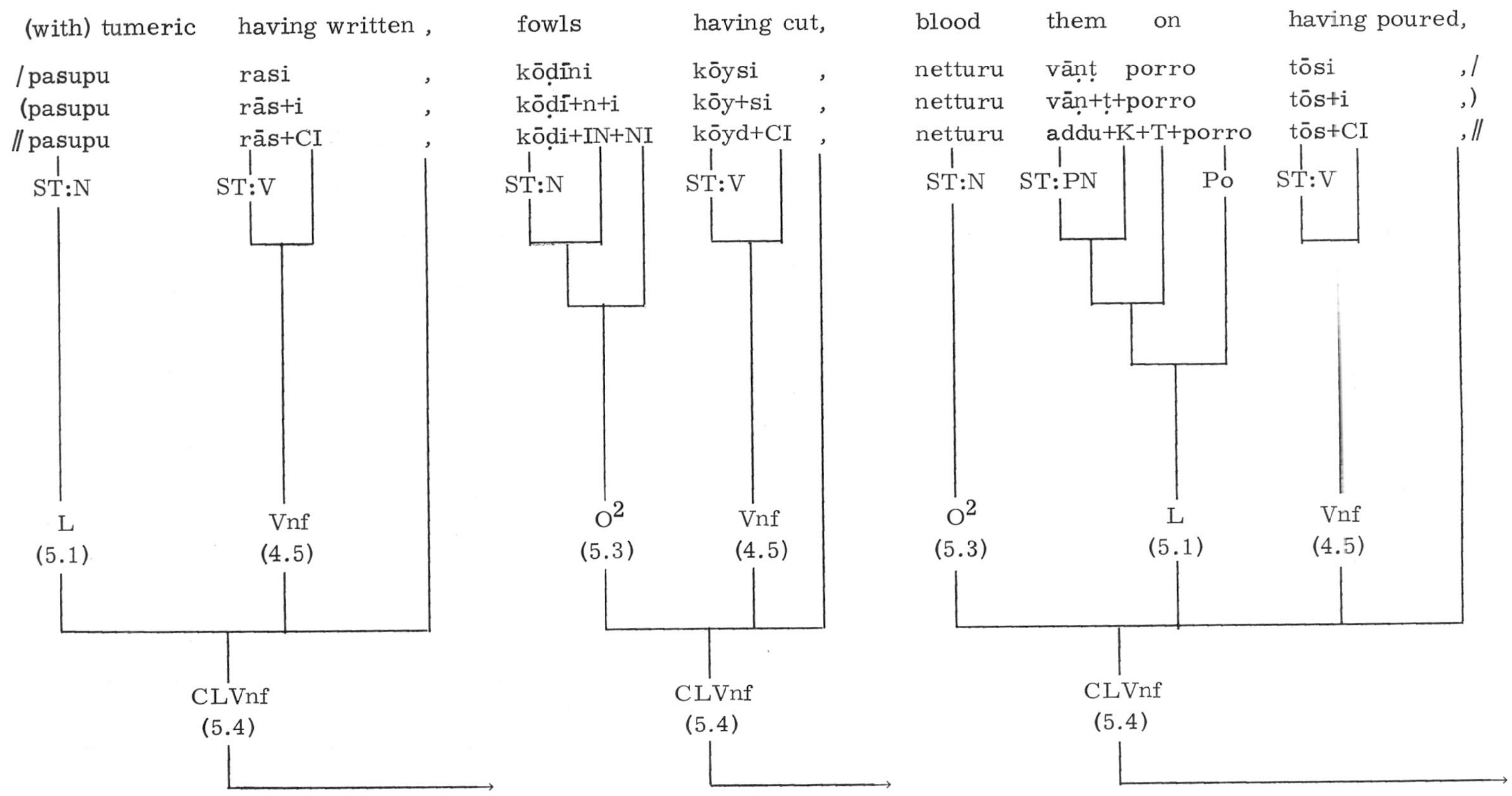
(with) tumeric having written , fowls having cut, blood them on having poured,
/pasupu rasi , kōḍīni kōysi , netturu vāṇṭ porro tōsi ,/
(pasupu rās+i , kōḍī+n+i kōy+si , netturu vāṇ+ṭ+porro tōs+i ,)
//pasupu rās+CI , kōḍi+IN+NI kōyd+CI , netturu addu+K+T+porro tōs+CI ,//
ST:N
ST:V
ST:N
ST:V
ST:N
ST:PN
Po
ST:V
L (5.1)
Vnf (4.5)
O2 (5.3)
Vnf (4.5)
O2 (5.3)
L (5.1)
Vnf (4.5)
CLVnf (5.4)
CLVnf (5.4)
CLVnf (5.4)

4. (continued)

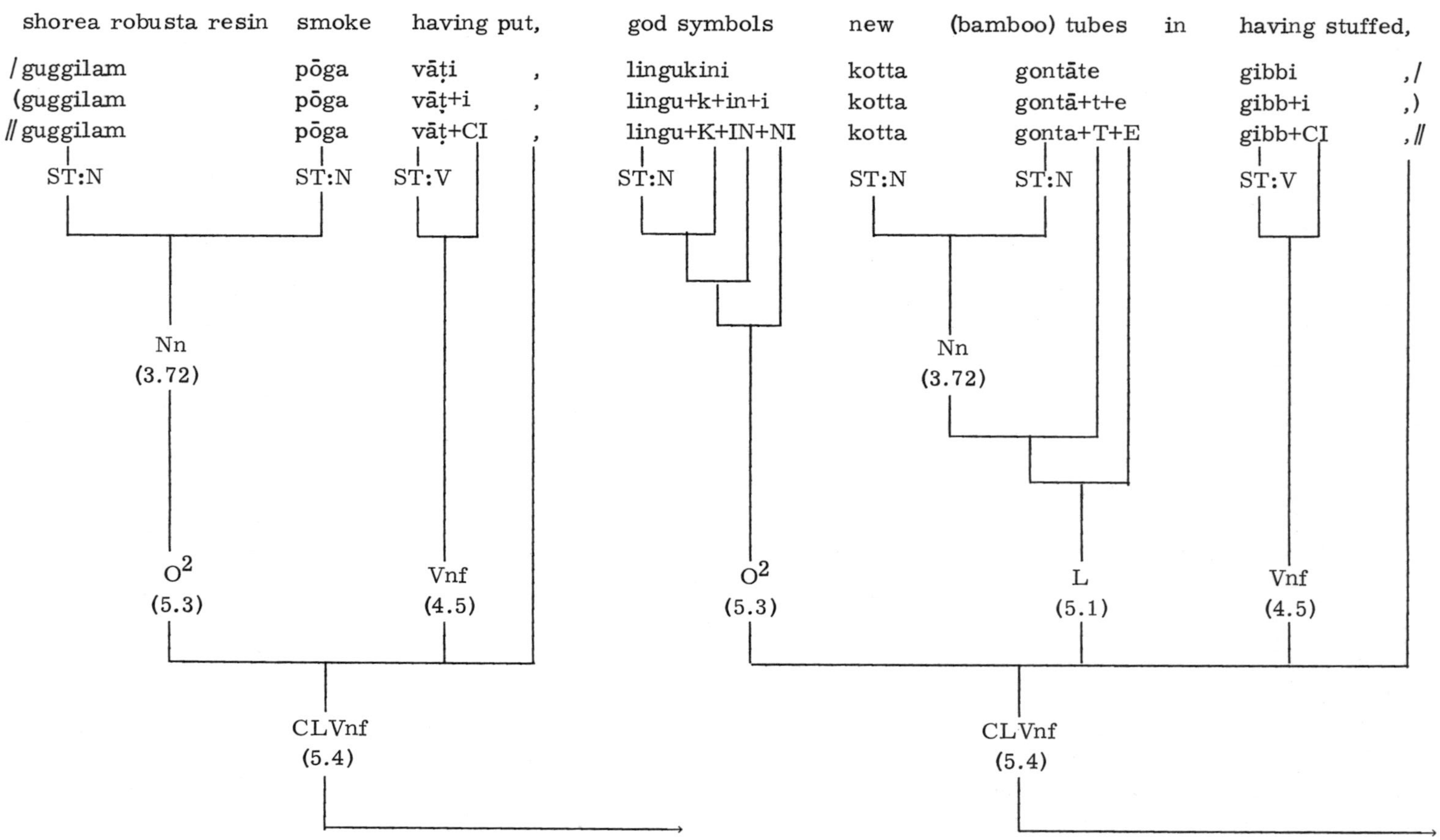
shorea robusta resin
smoke
having put,
god symbols
new
(bamboo) tubes
in
having stuffed,
/guggilam pōga vāṭi , lingukini kotta gontāte gibbi ,/
(guggilam pōga vāṭ+i , lingu+k+in+i kotta gontā+t+e gibb+i ,)
//guggilam pōga vāṭ+CI , lingu+K+IN+NI kotta gonta+T+E gibb+CI ,//
ST:N
ST:N
ST:V
ST:N
ST:N
ST:N
ST:V
Nn
(3.72)
Nn
(3.72)
O2
(5.3)
Vnf
(4.5)
O2
(5.3)
L
(5.1)
Vnf
(4.5)
CLVnf
(5.4)
CLVnf
(5.4)

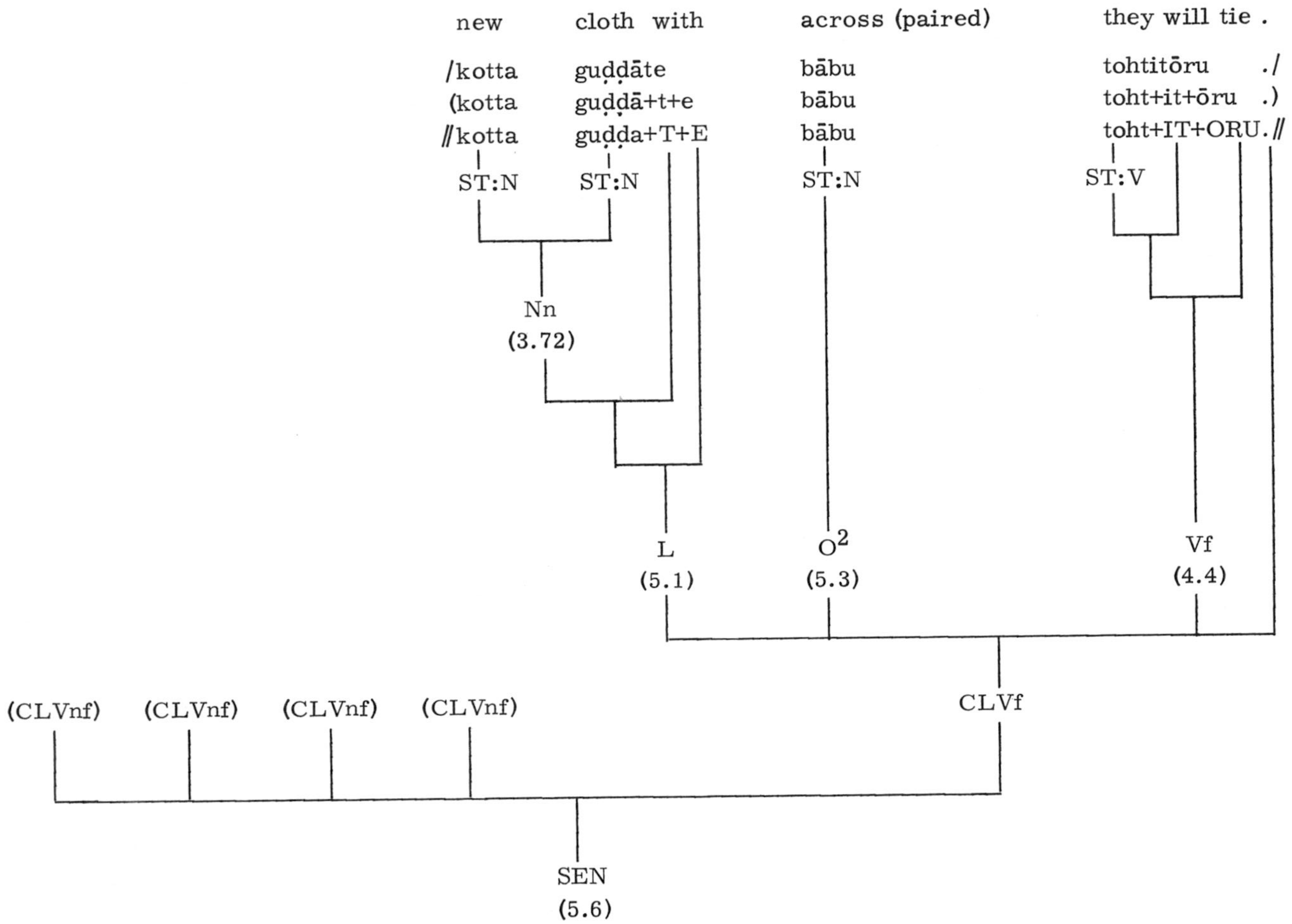
new
cloth with
across (paired)
they will tie .
/kotta
guḍḍāte
bābu
tohtitōru ./
(kotta
guḍḍā+t+e
bābu
toht+it+ōru .)
//kotta
guḍḍa+T+E
bābu
toht+IT+ORU.//
ST:N
ST:N
ST:N
ST:V
Nn
(3.72)
L
(5.1)
O2
(5.3)
Vf
(4.4)
(CLVnf)
(CLVnf)
(CLVnf)
(CLVnf)
CLVf
SEN
(5.6)

APPENDIX B

MORPHEME COVER SYMBOLS

In the body of the grammar, major grammatical elements were given with appropriate cover symbols and written in upper case letters within // //. Certain minor elements such as derivative suffixes and adverbial suffixes were introduced without cover symbols. In the following alphabetic list these elements are given as they appear initially in the grammar. They are listed together with an English gloss and reference to the section of the grammar in which they are discussed.

A	adjective suffix	4.6 (9)
AA	imperative singular personal ending	4.7
ADA	first person plural inclusive personal ending	4.7
-āḍi	derivative suffix	3.12
AK	potential tense mode	4.6
-akka	derivative suffix	3.16
AKU	third person fem./neut. personal ending	4.7
-āl	derivative suffix	3.11
-al(a)	adjective suffix	3.75
AMA	first person pl. excl. personal ending	4.7
-amma	derivative suffix	3.15
AN	infinitive	4.6
ANA	first person singular personal ending	4.7
ANI	habitual adjective suffix	4.6
-anna	adjective suffix	3.56, 3.75
ATAM	gerund	4.6
ATI	imperative plural personal ending	4.7
-atta	adjective suffix	3.75
-ayya	derivative suffix	3.14
-c	transitive suffix	4.3
CI	past participle suffix	4.6
CORE	present participle suffix	4.6
E	third person fem./neut. personal ending	4.7
E	instrumental-locative case suffix	3.46
-gā	adverb suffix	3.77
-ht	transitive suffix	4.3
I	genitive suffix	3.42, 3.75
IKI	dative case suffix	3.44
ILL	negative suppletive verb stem	4.9
IN	oblique suffix	3.41
-inā	adverb suffix	3.77
INI	second person singular personal ending	4.7
-ip	transitive suffix	4.3
IRI	second person singular personal ending	4.7

-is	transitive suffix	4.3
-is	causative suffix	4.3
IT	non-past tense-mode suffix	4.6
K	plural suffix	3.40
KANNA	concessive suffix	4.6
KASI	ablative case suffix	3.47
konn	defective and reflexive verb	4.9
KU	conditional suffix	4.6
kūḍadu	negative auxilliary verb	4.9
kuntā	negative participle	4.9
M	negative imperative mode suffix	4.6
mandi	plural numeral suffix	3.54
minn	suppletive verb	4.9
NI	accusative case suffix	3.45
O	negative tense mode suffix	4.6
-o	derivative suffix	3.6
ONDU	third singular masculine personal ending	4.7
ORU	third plural masculine personal ending	4.7
ORU	plural suffix	3.40
PE	personal ending	4.7
-pp	transitive suffix	4.3
-s	transitive suffix	4.3
T	oblique suffix	3.41
-t	transitive suffix	4.3
TI	nominalizing suffix	3.54, 3.79
TT	past tense mode suffix	4.6
TONTE	sociative-instrumental case suffix	3.48
-uṇḍu	derivative suffix	3.13
-ūru	derivative suffix	3.10
vaccu	defective verb	4.8
VAKE	negative participle suffix	4.6
VALAS	defective verb	4.9
-vi	nominalizing suffix	3.79
voddu	prohibitive	4.9
vūru	plural numeral suffix	3.54

Appendix C

CONSTRUCTION CLASSES

The following is an alphabetical listing of construction classes. Each item is provided with a descriptive label and reference to the section of the grammar in which it is analyzed.

Ab	ablative	(3.47), 5.3
Adj.	adjective	3.74
Adv	adverb	3.76
CL	clause	5.4
Cl	clitic	3.80
CLAdv	adverb clause	5.4
CLVnf	non finite verb clause	5.4
CLVf	finite verb clause	5.4
Con	connective	3.80
ConPH	connective phrase	5.5
D. Adj.	demonstrative adjective	3.74
Ew	echo word	3.72 (9)
Fi	filler	3.80
In	interjection	3.80
InPH	interjectory phrase	5.5
L	locative	(3.46), 5.1
N	noun	3.1
Nn	expanded noun	3.72
NPH	noun phrase	5.4
O	object	5.1
O^1	dative	(3.44), 5.1
O^2	accusative	(3.45), 5.1, 5.3
PH	phrase	5.5
PN	pronoun	3.56
Po	postposition	3.49
RPH	response phrase	5.5
S	subject	5.1
Sc	sociative instrumental	(3.48), 5.1
SEN	sentence	5.6
ST	stem (the noun or verb base)	3.1, 4.1
Tw	time word	(3.76), 5.2
V	verb	4.1
Vf	finite verb	4.4
Vnf	non finite verb	4.5
Vv	expanded verb	4.10

BIBLIOGRAPHY

Burrow, T., and S. Bhattacharya

1960. A comparative vocabulary of the Gondi dialects. Journal of the Asiatic Society (Calcutta), 2(2,3,4):73-251.

Cain, Reverend J.

1875. Native customs in the Godavari District. Indian Antiquary, 4:197-198.

1876. The Bhadrachallam Taluq, Godavari District, South India. Indian Antiquary, 5:357-359.

1879. The Bhadrachallam and Rekapalli Taluqas. Indian Antiquary, 8:33-36.

1881. The Koi, a southern tribe of the Gond. Journal of the Royal Asiatic Society, 13:410-414.

c. 1881. The Kois. MSS.

Emeneau, M. B.

1955. Kolami, a Dravidian Language. University of California Publications in Linguistics, vol. 12.

Fürer-Haimendorf, C. von

1945. The Reddis of the Bison Hills. London:Macmillan.

1948. The Raj Gonds of Adilabad. London:Macmillan.

Grigson, W. V.

1938. The Maria Gonds of Bastar. London:Oxford University Press.

India, Government

1942. Census of India, 1941, vol. 23, pt. 1, Madras:Government Press.

Mitra, A.

1964. Census of India 1961, vol. 1, pt. II-C language tables. Delhi, Manager of Publications.

Prasad, R. C.

1950. Koya mythology. Eastern Anthropologist, 14:160-165.

Tyler, Stephen A.

1964. Koya kinship: the relation between rules and behavior. Unpublished Ph.D. dissertation, Stanford University.

1965. Koya language morphology and patterns of kinship behavior. American Anthropologist, 67:1428-1440.

Yeatts, M. W. W.

1932. Census of India, 1931, vol. 14, pt. 2. Madras:Government Press.